OVER 60
AND
PICKING
UP SPEED

C. ELLEN WATTS

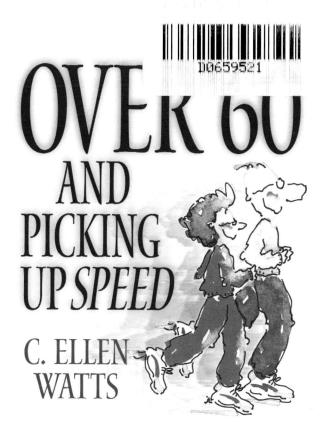

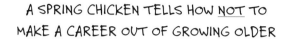

A SPRING CHICKEN TELLS HOW <u>NOT</u> TO
MAKE A CAREER OUT OF GROWING OLDER

OVER 60
AND
PICKING
UP *SPEED*

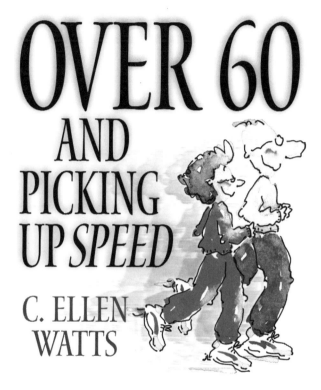

C. ELLEN
WATTS

PROMISE
PRESS
An Imprint of Barbour Publishing

Member of the
Evangelical Christian
Publishers Association

Printed in the United States of America.

Dedication

For my sisters, Alice, Elsie, and June—
growing older is now irrevocably us!
Thanks for modeling for me
how not *to make a career of it.*

Part 1

ADJUSTMENT COMES WITH THE DISCOUNT

The fool folds his hands and ruins himself.
Better one handful with tranquillity than
two handfuls with toil and chasing after the wind.
ECCLESIASTES 4:5–6

Expected Shelf Life

By the time 80 percent of our sixteen grandchildren had been promoted from the church nursery to my Sunday school class, my get-up-and-go had started to sit down and sulk. When creativity began taking weekly vacations, I did what every red-blooded layperson assumes is kosher.

I whined to the pastor.

I should have known he was too near the starting edge of his prime to recognize an energy crisis, let alone solve one. He listened attentively, suggested that every task has its days of discouragement, and said I was too young to retire from my position as Director of Children's Ministries. Then he asked me, "Would you really be happy if an inexperienced person stepped into your overworked shoes?"

It took me something like thirty-two years to muddle through my own inexperience and another ten to gain expertise. Still, I figured I'd like to give our church's energetic baby boomers a try.

Unfortunately, when I broached the subject to them, three said they were too busy, a fourth didn't do Sundays, and the rest explained that high tech and the world of television made it hard to relate to fellows like Moses. All had kids under my supervision. Not one responded with an offer to pray about the matter.

If the young were dreaming dreams after too much Letterman, who was left to mind the kids besides me? Although I had developed an incurable hearing problem and a roomful of happy children had started to sound like the Chipmunks singing backward, I could not bring myself to quit teaching until God (and my husband's employer) decided the time had come for us to move elsewhere.

Interestingly, once I was no longer available, not one but two of those boomers stepped in to teach my Sunday school class. These "inexperienced persons" so furthered God's ministry that I gladly concur with Edmund Burke when he said, "The arrogance of age must submit to being taught by youth."

Still, with a heart geared to service, how can you know

when it's time to let go and start trusting the next generation with the tasks you so love? For some, relinquishment may not come until late in life. The rest of us who have skidded past sixty should probably look for clues. For instance, it could be time to retire when:

- A new method or idea tires rather than tantalizes.
- Unlike the Energizer battery, you can no longer keep going and going.
- In your mind, the board meeting benediction and the bell that indicates the end of Sunday school are both equal to the dropping of manna.
- There becomes only one way to do things—yours.
- Your grown children insist.
- Like Elijah, you feel overworked and all alone, and a good night's sleep no longer helps.
- You wonder why meetings can't be scheduled for afternoon, preferably at your house, after naps.
- You've championed a responsibility for so long you think no one else cares.
- Stuff like stairs and bifocals and running out of Ben-Gay makes it difficult to function.
- You've been confronted by common sense.

The list is by no means exhaustive; nor is it an excuse for doing nothing. While I can no longer afford to physically burn midnight—and the Sunday school department's —oil, having one bum ear in no way stills the Voice that calls for daily obedience. There's plenty left to be done in this needy old world, and I can still do something.

FOOD FOR THOUGHT

Malcolm Muggeridge once said, "One of the pleasures of old age is giving things up." Although I'm a ways yet from old age, I've started to experience those pleasures. Still, all things considered, isn't shelf life really for lifers, not loafers? As long as we're still here, I expect God still has a use for us.

Time Was

A funny thing happened to time on my way to my word processor this morning. As I sashayed past the notebook where I try to jot my daily to-dos, I noticed that a whole lot of yesterday's list had leapfrogged itself over into tomorrow. Furthermore, whether due to procrastination, inertia, or both, half of the tasks I'd assigned to today were already destined for the middle of "whenever."

For a time, "The hurrieder I go, the behinder I get," seemed a clever little easy-out motto for others. Those words meant nothing to me. Now I may as well hang them in plastic around my neck. All but the hurry part. Claiming to hurry at this point of my life is but lip service.

In fact, thinking about what all I used to get done in a day makes me want to take a nap. The nap tendency, if acted upon, can of course zap away a good portion of my time. Who knows what becomes of the rest?

My personal overall time chart runs somewhat parallel to the first day of creation: Night and day started out pretty much the same. Sleep happened only through necessity when there was nothing more interesting left for me to do. Since I required only minimum amounts of sleep, the time in my day was unlimited by such trivialities as daylight.

Darkness and light became separated for me after the birth of our first child—and then only because she knew the difference. Days and nights finally gained a semblance of order following the entrance of the Greater Light who, for nearly five decades, has governed my life. When I gave my life to God, time became a vehicle I used for His service. I could pray with David, " 'You are my God.' My times are in your hands" (Psalm 31:14–15).

So why am I now at such a loss for time? And why do the Scriptures contain so few "time" verses that speak to my need? Even Solomon, in all his wisdom, deals mostly in generalities.

The truth is, slowing down is as natural to growing older as haste is to the young. We who were never troubled by time shortage before now need to examine our to-do lists and scratch off those entries that are no longer realistic. I, of course, must begin with the fact that these days I know the difference between day and night. If I choose to stay up past what has become my bedtime, I will not be painting woodwork or mucking out the refrigerator. More likely, I will be curled up in my favorite chair, my sleepy attention snagged by some book.

A second truth is this: Growing older includes circumstances not necessarily of our making—and these circumstances make change imperative. No mathematician need tell me, for example, that maintaining close relationships in a family grown to thirty takes more time than did our original nuclear unit, especially after those born into our household married and moved out. By the same token, meals with a retired spouse take more of my time than did my old habit of laying a peanut-buttered bagel alongside my word processor.

While only those with large families will grasp the full implications of the first illustration, and singles' households may not understand the time difference alluded to in the second, we are all, sooner or later, like it or not, going to have to deal with the fact that time seems to be shrinking annually from its former dimensions.

FOOD FOR THOUGHT

According to Steven Wright, "There's a fine line between fishing and standing on the shore looking like an idiot." Wise man, Steven Wright. Wiser yet, my daughter, who often asks her children, "If you don't have time to do it right, when will you have time to do it over?" Considering my current rate of speed, I won't have time. Could be that my ongoing frustration with time leaves me looking a little like Wright's you-know-what.

Better to take my daughter's advice. After all, if I am to spend the rest of my life in slow motion, I might as well use my time wisely and get the job done right.

Ice Pick

Figure skater Kurt Browning bowed out near the beginning of a short program and lost his chance of winning a million-dollar prize. A television cameraman caught Browning's sheepish expression and held his camera steady as Browning mouthed, "I forgot." Before long, the world knew the story that made ice competition history.

Browning's troubles began with his failure to practice systematically through steps he had once skated routinely. Unaware that months of showbiz performances had dulled his response to routine, Browning made a mistake early in his program, skated aimlessly for a moment, then did what no other figure skating champion had ever before done. He quit.

Scott Hamilton, on the other hand, skated what might

well have been a perfect 6.0. But Hamilton's days of competition were about to come to an end. Ignoring stern judges, he flashed his fans a grin and did a quick back flip, a definite no-no. While scores plummeted, the crowd went wild and a satisfied Hamilton collected flowers all the way to the locker room.

The diverse behavior of those young guys has left me with questions. Most of my life, I've looked at routine as a simple fact of life—but Browning's mess-up and Hamilton's intentional messing with routine all but yanked my imaginary skates out from under me.

Browning lacked the discipline he needed to stick to his routine—but Scott Hamilton simply decided to dispense with it for the pure joy of a greater freedom. So I wonder: Does my habitual brown toast with wheat shreds dredged through skim milk really have anything to do with healthier eating? Or does it have more to do with never having to come up with a plan before breakfast? Worse yet, is it simply habit (rather than any desire to listen from our pastor's "best side") that sends me sashaying from Sunday school class to the same east pew every Lord's Day?

Actually, our settling for a same general location each week began with good reason: The small fries could sight us more quickly following the benediction, which of course meant they could tackle Grandma and Grandpa that much faster. This stick-to-the-same-location principle now helps me find my glasses and parked car; if I can see the object in question, well, then I can "remember" where I left it. So many of my routines are simply based on convenience.

On the other hand, though, anyone who has ever lived near a mud road knows what ruts can do after a big freeze. Maintaining routine while bouncing all over the place is a little like this old couplet:

> *Habit with some must be a test of truth;*
> *It has to be right; they've done it since youth.*

So, one Sunday morning, I deliberately changed my path. While no one offered a million-dollar prize and my view of the pastor's profile dropped to so-so, hymn books were plentiful and the strange pew was comfortable. On my way out of church, since my routine contacts were all busy greeting one another in the east aisle, I smiled and shook hands with a young fellow who looked as if he could use the Lord, a mom, or a wife—in that order and maybe all three. Detecting no flicker of interest on his part in acquiring a grandmother, I quickly introduced him to a couple of fellows skilled in befriending—and then I slipped away via that unfamiliar aisle.

FOOD FOR THOUGHT

All things considered, probably routine is a good
plan to go for so long as you opt once in awhile
for flowers—like Hamilton—and never pull a
Browning by allowing your ruts to freeze.

Caller I.D.

When I measure my painful tussles with electronic gadgetry against the apostle Paul's affliction, it occurs to me that the prick of a thorn could hardly have been more invasive than what presently goes on in the name of modern technology.

Change seldom bothers me—but things that run or plug in do. Most days, my epitaph might likely read:

> *The poor dear's end*
> *Proved swift and clean.*
> *She clashed head-on*
> *With a machine.*

Consider the confusion caused by the telephone alone

—and then go with me to Philippi and picture this:

Following a severe flogging, Paul is thrown bodily into prison. Unable to sleep, he prays and sings all night, gets hit by an earthquake, and then wins his jailer to the Lord before walking away from his cell a free man. Dead on his feet, he registers a complaint concerning the flogging, then pulls a cellular from his tunic.

He's got Lydia's number recorded in memory because the fabric merchant, a new convert, has said Paul may use her guest room whenever he hikes into town. Unfortunately, the voice that answers is not Lydia's, but seems to rise from a tuna fish can: "If you wish to speak to a salesperson, press 1. If you wish to speak to someone in amethystine dyes, press 2." And so on through the eight-choice maze to "If you need assistance, press the pound sign."

Dazed and shaken, faint from lack of sleep, Paul wonders, "Pound who? Alex Bell? Or the dodo who crossed wires with a once-heralded invention?"

Now imagine this scene:

After a long day of shimming up sagging Silician churches, Paul takes a moment before hitting the sack to get Barnabas on the horn to talk about Cyprus. In the middle of what sounds like a good report struggling through a bad connection, as if he has no clue that Paul's long-distance calls must be paid for with missionary offerings, Barnabas says, "Oops, got another call coming in."

On hold, Paul prays for patience and hangs onto his cool while the magic contraption allows him to hold his cake of friendship and nibble its edges, too.

"That was John Mark," Barny says. "Poor kid's been homesick, begging again to go home. . . . Paul? Paul? Is it this crazy connection? Or did I hear you counting?"

Paul hits the off button, tries for a better connection, and is informed by Tuna Tones that Barny's voice mail is full.

Along about now, if this were really happening, Paul would likely be begging the Lord to

please take the dumb phone and give back
his thorn.

As for me, already this morning, I have said no in
assorted decibels to a Florida miss soliciting funds for an
airlift from the eye of a Midwestern tornado that happened three weeks ago. Twice today I've hung up at the
unmistakable sound of a computerized ad refusing to kick
in. I don't know what Paul's "thorn" was—but could it
really be worse than mine?

FOOD FOR THOUGHT

Despite that pesky thorn, the Lord continued to
use assorted people and innovative methods to
supply Paul's needs. For all my complaints, I
know God looks after me just as carefully. He
knows that the telephone is what keeps me in
touch with my loved ones. And even though my
word processor betrays me at inopportune times,
He's confirmed its necessity. What's more, He
knows who stood with the shortest supply as He
handed out patience.

Early on, when I begged Him for extra patience, He blessed me with children; and when patience again lagged, He replenished it through grandchildren. Since succeeding generations will most likely not be mine to tend, the Lord has obviously devised a new plan for granting me patience.

But why has He chosen to nourish my aging patience with changes that so invade my space? Why machines? The clue, I suppose, is the same as with grandbabies: When you're done changing, as the saying goes, you're done altogether. Since I'm not done with life yet, I'd best resign myself to change.

Remedial Remedies

If deceased loved ones can look down from heaven and observe us folks down below, my mother has probably been doubled over the balcony rail laughing her head off since Sunday.

I used to scoff at her remedies.

- Burn a tuft of sheep's wool on the bottom of a flat iron and use the oily residue to cure a wart.
- Boil a pot of onions with a whole lot of sugar to make loblolly cough syrup.
- Cover a chest smeared with odiferous grease with gray flannel; safety pin the flannel to your long johns until either the cough disappears or you get to change into summer underwear.

I never put much stock in any of these cures. But last Sunday I was desperate.

I had wanted to be at my best, and here I was with a two-day sinus headache claiming squatter's rights behind my temple.

"I know just the remedy." This was not my mother speaking, but my daughter. The remedy, it seems, had been handed down by an older sister who declared it worked.

Since those two had been masters since childhood at rejecting my remedies, I figured this one must be a winner or she would never have dared mention it to me. So against my better judgment, I listened to what she had to say.

That night, the headache was still with me while I polished off two bowls of Sunday night popcorn. I said to my husband, Norm, "I am about to do something really gross."

"Mmm," came from behind whatever book Norm was reading.

Gross, I know, is not always the same for men and boys as it is for ladies. I tried, again, to get his attention.

"What I'm about to do may look funny, but the girls said it would help my headache."

Still no answer. I realized I could not look to Norm to save me from my desperation. So I went to the kitchen to follow my daughter's instructions.

I sliced a trace of thin peel from an orange, rolled and inserted it into one nostril, and went back to my chair and my book. Three minutes later, my eyes had started to water, and my nose was on fire. I stuck it out for the full fifteen minutes as I had been told to do, while Norm remained discreetly behind his book.

Midway through the second half of the treatment, I dropped my own book. What was I doing with orange peel up my nose when I have a low tolerance to citrus fruit, especially when served in the peel? Desperation can drive you to do some pretty foolish things.

FOOD FOR THOUGHT

That orange peel made cracks in my nose that took forever to heal and remedied nothing. The pain got me thinking on fissures of a different sort—the divisions within our churches.

I'm for whatever it takes to bring folks to Christ—but we don't have to let desperations drive us to foolishness. There are some tried and true remedies for getting a church off its sick bed and back into action:

- Burn time in intercessory prayer, and allow the oil of the Holy Spirit to heal all that is unsightly.
- Bubble over into your community with your own personal good news, demonstrating a life made sweet by Jesus Christ, whose grace is sufficient and available to all.
- Cover your lifestyle with faithfulness until the penetrating vapors of service, commitment, and financial stewardship help you cough up the deep-seated selfishness that keeps you from the kind of discipleship that is winsome to others.
- Remember that preventive measures are better than remedies, and carefully nurture your children and youth by regularly teaching and modeling the Word.

Padded Cell

You may already have heard the story of the woman who was hoping to catch up with her husband on his way home from work, so she dialed his cell phone number. He answered on the first ring. From a few feet away. From their own garage. The story may well be a sign of our times.

Having not the slightest desire yet to own one more preprogrammed device hardly qualifies me to pass judgment on a thingamajig teensy enough to hide in a handbag. Or to censor a tool that may be no more than a status symbol to some but tremendously helpful to others. Still, I cannot resist sharing from an ever growing repertoire of cell phone remarks:

- "Let me call you back on a real phone. They

don't cost anything."
- "I never give my cell number to people I might not want to talk to."
- "Here's my cell phone number, but I'd rather you not use it."
- "It's great being able to take care of business and drive at the same time."

Whoa! In which lane? Yours? Mine? Or the center line? While cinching a deal after a traffic light turns green, causing Michelins to cool and motorists to ignite in your wake?

Furthermore, I don't care a fig how trendy it may be to visit with friends while driving the babies to a sitter. A cell phone sprouting from the ear of a commuter with one or more kids in or out of seat belts and car seats is a hazard.

And who among those of us who would rather leave tips than cook has never been interrupted in the middle of an entrée by jingles coming from the right, the rear, and the hip pocket of a cowboy sliding into the booth on the left?

The signals, praise be, are pleasantly discreet. But when an old gal like me, with a hearing problem and no hearing aid, can tune into baby-sitting instructions given two tables away and hear every decibel, it's time somebody out there in 'tronicsland tinkered less with this latest space-invading device and more with human volume. Maybe stuff a manners pamphlet into each box before the phone leaves the factory?

There was a time when telephones hung attached to a wall, and lots of folks never owned one. If you had something to say, you traveled to wherever a telephone happened to be, said it, and hung up. What's more, it took a crank to run one. Eventually, of course, came the desk phone, the kitchen phone, and the phone that awakens in the middle of the night.

With the advent of the long cord, the telephone became a time zapper. Housewives could now accomplish two tasks at once. Later on came the cordless, and the rest of the world, if they stayed within range, could do likewise. Human beings had achieved a new standard of communication.

You want to know what I think? I think that the God who made us with one mind and two hands must have looked down at all our hurry-scurry and said to Himself, "Silly people. Can't find ways fast enough to take on multiple duties so they can complain over being too busy. I can fix that. I'll give them still one more toy. This toy, however, will be different. This little baby must come with a guarantee that, for 24 hours a day, 7 days a week, 365 days a year, vacation or no—for the rest of a lifetime, in fact—human

31

beings will perpetually and without let-up have power in purse or pockct to talk to people at the same time they're doing anything else in the world."

So you tell me. Is the cell phone a gift from God—or a curse?

FOOD FOR THOUGHT

The trouble with any gizmo designed to interrupt folks in the middle of a shower is that it can also be heard in church. Unlike the wee golden bells on the garb of Old Testament priests, even the merriest of electronic melodies tends to short-circuit a sermon.

Big Deal

There are those of us who remember when, if you ran out of nails, you got in your car, drove to the hardware store, walked a few steps, bought your nails, retraced your steps, drove home, and got on with your project. The same worked for calf meal and corn plasters. Not anymore.

When big-time developers first came out with malls, outfitted them with stairs and escalators, and planted public rest rooms along barren, two-kilometer halls, I thought we'd seen it all. Supposedly you could get it all at the mall.

Maybe so. But who in their right mind wants to carry it? Half a day of Christmas shopping for my big family means multiple trips to where I hope I parked the car. Either that, or they let me inside with the pickup.

Because you can't really buy it all at the mall, the advent

of the super center, I suppose, was inevitable. Inevitable, perhaps, but I'm here to tell you that while one-stop shopping sounds good, one size does not necessarily fit all. For sure, the super center is no place for folks held together with back braces and support hose. Not when the item you need lies hidden along a thirty-aisle maze of unmarked passages.

Try juggling a decorated birthday cake alongside one giant beach ball, a pair of fourteen-inch tires, and a small carton of guppies, and those super-sized carts aren't so great either. Jiggle one all the way to row F8 of a super-sized parking lot, fail to find the blue Ford Taurus with the dent in its hood, rattle over a few more acres of blacktop, and you'd fake apoplexy or break a leg just to get a chance at one of those stalls marked by a wheelchair.

You think I'm exaggerating? Read on.

"This won't take long," I promised my spouse who hates to shop.

So, since neither of us had visited our latest edge-of-town monstrosity, he decided to go along. That was his mistake.

My mistake had to do with a false assumption: Surely a simple list of everyday items could get us through the fast lane and back out to the car before my long-suffering mate could ask, "How long is long?"

Item #1 on my list was sold out, so I plowed on through a couple of hundred carts and kids, counted aisles as best I could, and found item #2 on aisle 17. From there, aisles 20 and 23 should have been a cinch. Not so. When I finally caught up with a salesperson stocking shelves on aisle 12, she said, "Sorry, we don't carry those here." She did, however, point me toward the fifth and final item on my list.

Exactly forty-seven minutes later, we left that not-so-super center with one small bag in hand. Seven blocks from home, we stopped at a homely little variety store that has occupied the same small strip mall for as long as we can remember. The items we needed were all in stock and in plain sight, aisles 2 and 4.

The cashier offered a cheery, "Thank you. Come again," and then looked puzzled as we chorused, "Believe us, we will!"

FOOD FOR THOUGHT

Even the church has joined in the size race; these days, apparently you need a guide to get you to where you're supposed to be more than you need a Sunday school teacher once you get there. For those of us who grew up in an earlier era, this current romance with stupendous size smacks of the ridiculous. The dimensions of our church buildings will never be as important as the old-fashioned human touch. After all, good things come in small packages.

First Chair

"There are two kinds of sound—music and noise," I used to say to our kids whenever the decibel count of whatever they were listening to upstaged conversation and demolished my sanity. Whenever I practiced piano as a kid, my parents sang the same song, different verse.

"Don't pound."

"I'm not," I always said. Then, as my chubby forefinger stumbled onto the next right note, I would get all excited and hit the key hard to be sure.

With this in mind, you can well imagine my confusion during my first visit to an old-fashioned camp meeting after the pianist attacked each stanza with the power of a steamroller in high gear and everyone said, "Wasn't she great?"

Perhaps it's my age, but I still scratch my head at

times over some of what goes on in the name of music. Likewise the flap that surrounds it.

My first introduction to the possibility that all minds are not necessarily in tune on the subject of church music came at age nine during Vacation Bible School. Following opening exercises in the sanctuary, an innovative leader suggested we sing a chorus as we trooped to our basement classrooms.

The chorus began with, "God has blotted them out. . . ." The song spoke happily of freedom that comes from sins forgiven, included a Scripture reference (Isaiah 44:22–23), and ended with a rousing, "And now I can shout, for that means me!"

It was the shouting part that got us in trouble.

Seems someone took issue with our being told to shout "shout" at the top of our noisy little lungs. What my fourth-grade heart understood as joyous proclamation, some sour saint believed to be irreverent, and we were only allowed to sing that fun song twice.

Kind of makes one wonder what the lady's reaction might have been thirty years later to "If you're saved and you know it, stomp your feet."

My Quaker heritage may be partly to blame, but I like things quiet. I like my music, if not quiet, at least to be in good taste. In my modest musical opinion, a worship band offers no more reason to cringe than does some Olympic-geared organist going for the crescendo gold.

Striving to help keep the peace during this ongoing sanctuary version of musical chairs, however, takes more than a vote for variety. It takes wisdom. Obviously not mine, for I felt pretty hard-pressed for a response the day a dear person leaned near and gave me her discreet opinion.

"I don't mind the trumpets," she said, "but do you really think drums ought to be allowed in church?"

Even old Solomon might have gone slack-jawed. My grandson was playing them. And very well at that.

Matter of fact, I once played a little percussion myself.

FOOD FOR THOUGHT

We who are over sixty may well remember how, when our hearts were young and "gay" meant "carefree," any song short enough to be called a chorus was considered suspect. Now some of us who chafed over that tend to assume that all hard-to-decipher lyrics are also bad lyrics. We forget that our own songs were no better.

Surely this author could not have been alone in her struggle to understand the exact meaning behind popular old choruses like "Deep and Wide." And how could anyone in their teens following World War II ever forget a tongue-tangler like "Marezydoats"? What goes around comes around.

Shoptalk

The one who said, "If you want something badly enough, you can get it," is obviously neither my age nor has she gone shopping lately.

No place else in the world, and never before in a lifetime, have there been more stores and shops, malls and mini-malls, marts and markets, and overgrown outlets. Or stuff.

So, why can't we simply go buy what we need?

We will, if we can find one that fits.

Take shoes. I found some I liked, asked for 7B in black, and got offered multiple choice:

a. Purple.
b. 7½ C in taupe.
c. The "latest."

The "latest" being a style my fourteen-year-old grand-daughter would die for, I shook my head at all three and asked the salesperson to special order.

She couldn't. The manager had decided against carrying that brand, which made no sense. Not with half the ladies I know opting for shoes designed to carry us over the hill in both comfort and style. Besides, now that those in high places say they want to fix who knows what all for the Medicare crowd, you would think they would want to see us properly clothed.

Instead, we get teensy little skirts that couldn't hide a varicose vein if they met one, and a good-looking dress is a thing of the past.

Clotheswise, since they don't give a hoot if they all look alike, men fare better. They face the same predicament as women, however, when it comes to all the junk planted under the name of merchandise to keep folks from finding what they need from a store.

A screw falls down the register during the installation of a new switch plate. It's an ordinary screw, easily replaced, only, guess what? You can't buy just one. Packagers of nails and screws and such no longer consider it safe for singles to mingle in open bins. Never mind how many lifetimes it could take for forty-seven more switch plate screws to fall down the register. You buy a whole package, put the extras away, and, if a next time ever occurs, go buy another package because you can't remember where you put the forty-seven you already have.

Perhaps some have wondered along with me who buys some of the stuff that clogs store aisles, dangles from crowded spindles, and falls. Having been born at least sixty years too soon, there's no contest as to who picks up most of it. We can't help ourselves. Except when it comes to toy departments.

Those toy departments we once sashayed through for fun and for the sake of nostalgia have turned into plastic jungles no Medicard-carrying aunt, uncle, or grandparent should have to hack through. To get to where you're going, you wade through sinister-looking molded men, missiles, and space machines, monster mania, and a whole lot of other junk, plus more hyped-up dinosaurs than most care to believe ever existed. The stuff speaks, squeaks, roars, fires, flashes fire, bares teeth, and more. Some toys simply lie on the floor burning batteries and defying adults of all ages to dare depart carrying nothing other than one measly game of Candyland to show for the hassle.

Kind of makes one wonder how we ever managed with our baby dolls and balls and homemade slingshots.

Or even how our kids made it through childhood under the influence of plain old Tonka trucks and hula hoops.

But C. S. Lewis said, "All that is not eternal is eternally out of date." So if you look at it that way, then a whole lot of this world is pretty passé.

FOOD FOR THOUGHT

At least we have the privilege of living where shopping's an option. Might be I should prop up my tired feet and thank the Lord that all He asks me to wear at the moment is a garment of praise.

Part 2

FIDDLESTICKS FITNESS

A cheerful heart is good medicine,
but a crushed spirit dries up the bones.
PROVERBS 17:22

From Temple to Treadmill

When it comes to exercise, I'm with former U.S. president Harry S. Truman who said, "Take a two-mile walk every morning before breakfast. That way you can get it over with and get on with what you know you're going to like about your day."

Actually, of course, Mr. Truman didn't say that last part. The bit about getting it over with is my own philosophy. Having an alarm clock jerk me upright so I can splash cold water over my face, struggle into sweats, and hit the sidewalk while half the neighborhood is still asleep is not my idea of fun. Furthermore, having Norm do all this with a grin while he still manages to remember the house key is nothing short of galling. Of course Norm has a ninety-four-year-old mother who can still bend over and touch her tennies flat-handed.

By the time we have circled the park, I am starting to think about breakfast. I don't know why. I will not be fixing anything scrumptious like scrambled eggs and hot biscuits oozing with melted butter and marmalade. I will instead act as slave to the lower part of the triangle that has replaced the cartoons on the back of some cereal boxes. I may also think darkly of John the Baptist. You know, locusts and wild honey. In other words, fat and sugar, both items from the pointed little tip of the nutrition triangle. No-no's.

Or I may take heart when I remember my Civil War veteran friend and his idle son. Each morning, while the son lolled in a chair on the porch, the dapper old gentleman donned gray spats and took a long walk with the aid of an ebony cane. Always, at the end of his walk, he came into the meat market where I worked, where he would buy chicken or fish for their dinner. On Saturdays, he also bought a sizable, well-marbled steak to please his son. He chose his own small Sunday steak with care and instructed me to please trim the rest of the fat.

The son (they say) died in his chair on the porch at age forty-three with an empty potato chip bag in one hand and a half-eaten sausage in the other.

My veteran friend made it to the ripe old age of 108.

Could be that Arnold Glasgow was right when he said, "Your body is the baggage you must carry through life. The more excess baggage, the shorter the trip."

The truth is that while we all live in bodies that are constantly being vandalized by time, this whole business of doing what's healthy would be easier if God had zapped a few more commandments onto those stones along with the Big Ten—something like:

- Thou shalt have no breakfast until after thou hast walked.
- Thou shalt consume only those foods that sprout from the soil and that echo with the dry crunch of oats.
- Eight glasses of water shalt thou drink daily, that thy days may be long upon this earth and thy body free from that which would pollute.

FOOD FOR THOUGHT

Since we don't have direct instructions from God, we must each decide for ourselves what it means to keep our bodies from ruling our spirits.

In the Old Testament, Daniel sets a pretty good example—except, what would a pip-squeak teenager understand about addiction to butter pecan pie? Reality didn't hit *me* until after cholesterol claimed squatter's rights in my arteries.

Looking after our health needs can be especially discouraging to those of us for whom diet and exercise no longer seem to do much aesthetical good. Still, since a good deal of me has started to answer the call of gravity, a push back from the table and an early morning walk lends energy to my day and gives me a greater sense of well-being.

And if that isn't enough motivation to get me moving, I can take inspiration from the fact that Jesus never owned a Grand Marquis. He walked.

Maintenance

They say that shortly after a person grows to full stature, the body then begins to slowly shrink. While I have never checked this out, I do know that about the time I thought I had life all together, some of the stuff called me had already started to fall apart. In fact, before Norm and I could subscribe to *Modern Maturity,* maintenance had become an item in our budget.

My need to *maintain* happened a little like Carl Sandburg's fog: It came "on little cat feet," took one look at my birth date, and then moved in. Unlike the fog, it may never move on.

Once upon a time, we dealt with a dental must here and a doctor's order there. Now that we're both over sixty, however, the trappings to "do" our combined uppers and lowers take up more drawer space than last summer's T-shirts. Dental maintenance vies for time with morning devotions and the late-night news.

I never anticipated envying my parents. But those Pa and Ma bowls they filled nightly with soda water and what Dad referred to as "choppers" now seem so inexpensively simple. A cinch, in fact, when compared to all the threaders; mouthwash; super, waxed, and Teflon-coated floss; and the power-driven squirt gun prescribed by our dentist.

And our teeth aren't the only things we now struggle to maintain. Nestled among the dust bunnies on top of our refrigerator is a basket, not for Easter eggs, but for pills. Not life-or-death pills or lower-that-fever pills, but pills to thin, thicken, raise, lower, relieve, clear, supplement, and soothe. Pills enough to halt an airport security scanner in midroll.

Meanwhile, Norm invests in gimmicks for easing the back, and I pay extra for unscented everything. Thankfully, we are not yet enslaved by the bunion remedies, wristlets, wraps, and slings required by some who have made it to our same stage of physical disintegration. We do, however, depend on our pillows, which, some would argue, may not belong under "maintenance." Maintenance or no, if tucked just right, the faded blue denim cushion, the red flannel pillow, or the cushion sewn from old neckties can do wonders for our arthritis.

Further, while we don't need them all, there are probably enough labels ending with -ic, -um, -ine, -al, -ate, and other such suffixes in our medicine cabinet to stock a pharmacy. Throw in a few treadmills, rowing machines, and stationary bicycles, and you know that beyond-prime maintenance is big business.

While all or some of the above may come across as silly, doing whatever it takes to keep ourselves healthy is not. Preoccupation with health, however, is another matter. The minute we catch ourselves revolving around our aches and pains and toothbrushing, as if our wrinkling bodies should be ironed before we can possibly make it into heaven, we're in trouble. Especially if we neglect to maintain the part of us that will, for sure, endure for eternity. Given equal time, prayer can zap away dross from places super floss never dared enter.

FOOD FOR THOUGHT

Even after we've done our best to keep things in perspective, the time and money required to maintain bodies that refuse to cooperate can be discouraging. When that happens, it wouldn't hurt to remind ourselves that a cheerful heart just might do as much good as a whole kit full of medicine (see Proverbs 17:22).

Stone's Throw

Having one deaf ear has its advantages. I have read peacefully while a thousand Indianapolis 500 hopefuls "vroomed" across the tube. I've slept through hailstorms, jangling phones, and kids going barf in the night. And I've missed hearing a thrice-told joke. Still, since the ear is connected to the mouth by an auditory canal barely an inch-and-a-half long, and since the tongue occupies a good share of the mouth, having a bum ear can also lead to trouble.

My mother dealt regularly with a child she claimed came with a tongue "hinged in the middle and flapping at both ends." I blush to confess that child was me. "Hearing something," she often told me, "in no way obligates one to repeat it. In fact," she might add, "it often shows a fine command of the English language to say nothing."

Wow. I suspect a friend of mine wishes now she'd known that. "Guess what's in store for so-and-so?" she whispered as she sat next to me at a ladies' event.

I couldn't guess.

"She is going to be a you-know-what," my friend confided.

I had no problem decoding her meaning. Since my original you-know-what title has been multiplied by sixteen (once for each grandkid), and my friend is a great-you-know-what as well, we both knew that a you-know-what is a good thing to be.

My day being full, I soon excused myself from the event, thanked our hostess, and departed early. Halfway through the second stoplight, I remembered I'd intended to congratulate so-and-so concerning her impending you-know-whathood. Since it was too late for that (in reality, it was too early), I continued with my errands.

Later, at home, I reached for the ringing phone and recognized the voice of my friend.

"We who are hard of hearing should never repeat a word before having all the facts confirmed. I misheard what I overheard. Now I'm having to call and make my crooked path straight," she confessed. "It's not so-and-so who's going to become a you-know-what; it's what's-her-name!"

"No problem."

"Not for you maybe. But, my dear, I congratulated the wrong person! At least I only told two people."

Good taste, I could have told her, *is the ability to shut one's own mouth before somebody else does.*

Instead, as we laughed together over her harmless mistake, I couldn't help thinking, *There, but for a busy morning, go I, who could so easily have been the first to offer the mistaken congratulations.*

My friend worried on. "What if the words I overheard had been words that could have hurt someone?"

The gentle and gladsome bit of gossip repeated by my friend had not been unkind. In a very real sense, her words had to do with life. What's more, if what she had overheard had contained so much as a hint toward the vicious, I know beyond a doubt that, like my mom, she would have chosen to leave such a stone unthrown.

Still, we all need to remember Proverbs 18:21: "The tongue has the power of life and death."

FOOD FOR THOUGHT

My mother was the first to remind me that if I

couldn't say something good about a person, then I'd best say nothing at all. She would have liked the wise words of O. R. Card: "Among my most prized possessions are words that I have never spoken." Likely, Brothers Solomon (Proverbs) and James (chapter 3) would also have had her respect.

Since Mom never lost so much as a decibel of hearing, I guess I'm left with a choice. Either listen up and get my stories straight or keep whatever I think I heard to myself.

The same probably goes for my friend.

Paper Tale

I've discovered why folks begin longing for heaven the minute illness or pain forces their focus toward the physical. It's the paperwork.

Dr. A, of course, has seen us through flu shots and allergies, ingrown toenails, and cholesterol. Paperwork for his office begins and ends with a signed check.

This time, however, the problem was beyond Dr. A's expertise, so we made an appointment with Dr. B, who promptly gave us one blue, one pink, two yellow, and two white forms to complete. The paperwork could have been worse. All we had to remember was what my spouse had been up to twenty years ago on the day his problem began, how many times, and in what ways he had since been bothered. Stuff like that. Six pages to be exact. No, make that four. Two had to do with vitals, like where to send the bill.

Dr. B prodded, X-rayed, prescribed a relaxant, and sent Norm to Hospital #1 for further procedures. Arriving ten minutes before appointment time, for more than an hour we fought for comfort on a waiting room couch. About the time the second relaxant kicked in, the woman in charge produced several papers and curtly instructed Norm: "Fill these out."

Leaning heavily against the chest-high counter, my high school sweetheart tried; he really did. When I offered to help, he gave me a loopy stare and mumbled something to the woman, who stabbed at page one with a mauve-tipped fingernail and said tartly, "That should have been on this line."

While my spouse collapsed in the closest chair, I crossed out some lines, added others, scratched out a wobbly "X" from the box beside "single," and removed our old zip code from the tail end of our telephone number.

"Fill these out and take them along," warbled Dr. B when procedure results indicated a need to see Dr. C. By then, the effects of the relaxant had worn off; the patient, struggling for patience, was able to legibly and correctly write down answers to questions he had already answered both for Dr. B and Mauve Fingernails.

Ten miles away, the redhead commandeering the desk at Dr. C's office accepted the carefully completed pages and served my beloved with yet more forms. Norm barely made it through the seventh page before being summoned to Dr. C's inner sanctum.

"But I still have five pages to go. . . ."

The redhead shrugged. "No problem."

As my partner in life followed Dr. C's nurse, I fumed a little. If incomplete paperwork presented no problem, then why? . . .

Luckily, Dr. D's office was but two doors away. One would have thought two doctors sharing a common department could have divvied up the forms as well. But no.

Dr. D's papers, delivered by a buxom matron wearing a smock covered with miniature hot air balloons, proved identical to the ones my spouse had failed to complete for Dr. C. Later, as we were about to leave, she handed him two more.

"Fill these out so you won't have to deal with paperwork at the hospital," she said.

Hospital #2's outpatient waiting room was filled with reluctant scribes filling out endless forms. We waited until all personnel with clip-on I.D.s had their backs turned, and then we dropped our papers on the counter and hid behind a couple of last year's magazines.

But we couldn't escape. "Sir, if you'll please fill these out before we take you on back. . ."

One repeat hospital trip, a ream of paper, one more doctor, and several weeks of therapy later, it occurred to us that the Great Physician, like Dr. A who knows us so well, requires no paperwork.

FOOD FOR THOUGHT

It's no wonder ailing folks tend to hanker for heaven. God's healing is as simple as the gospel. All we have to do is rely on Christ.

Part 3

ANGELS AND ATTITUDES

All a man's ways seem right to him,
but the LORD weighs the heart.
PROVERBS 21:2

Wrinkles in Prime

There's nothing quite like a high school reunion for capturing a nostalgic and sometimes sobering view of how often we are shaped (sometimes literally!) by the way we live our lives.

The reunion wasn't a large event. I grew up in a town so small our class sponsor covered the empty chairs with lilacs the day our class filed into the front row of the Methodist church choir loft to receive our diplomas. When your community phone book is barely equal in size to the church bulletin, you do what you can to get a quorum. So not one, but several of our hometown's high school classes attended my reunion.

For kids who had warmed cold feet over the same coal furnace registers, we were a motley assortment. Popularity appeared to have changed hands—or fizzled. Not everyone destined most likely to succeed had done so, and some of the least likely had done well.

As I walked into the party, I couldn't help but think of a warning my mother often gave to kids who threw hissy fits: "What if your face should freeze that way?" Some of my former classmates looked as though their faces had indeed frozen, right in the midst of a tantrum. When we merge the way we were yesterday with what we are today, we may not always end up with a nicely preserved tomorrow. Some in the group who were hovering within easy dip of the chips, for instance, had flirted with cholesterol for a very long time.

I paused beside them to chat with a girl I remembered as having diligently "studied" *True Confessions* magazines behind carefully propped textbooks. Hired now to tend the library, she was under fire from her board for buying too heavily into paperback romance. As she chattered on about the sad reality of alumni divorces and illicit affairs, I excused myself to speak with the heroine of the school's softball history.

Her deeply lined face and the odor of tobacco smoke that hung over her like a shroud told me she had been fooled by the Kool's and Camels' lie. One oxygen tank and some pretty constant hacking from two other individuals helped identify other former classmates who had bought the same lie.

Avoiding the lonely bachelor (the guy nice girls were never allowed to date), I made myself walk over to a pain-riddled woman who had just settled herself into a chair with the aid of two canes. Having once shown her "affection" for me with a fist in my back, I found she had softened only slightly.

Not all were so difficult, of course. Along with farmers and homemakers, cousins and schoolteachers, I talked with the mayor of a small western city, and I recognized a well-dressed man who had once been too poor to own socks.

Spotting a short fellow with an infectious grin, I was in for a surprise. The school clown—the kid who had made us laugh in a world that was short on laughter when dads and brothers and sweethearts were off fighting World War II—had given his gift of gab to God; he was now in the ministry. Like me, he had been kept (more or less) out of trouble by church folks who cared enough to haul us to Sunday school. Having all grown up in the same town, though, probably every alumnus in that room had had our same chances at salvation. Those same kindly church people would have been more than happy to cart every one of us off to Sunday school, but not all of us were willing to go.

Horace was right: "The jar will long retain the fragrance of whatever it was steeped in when new." As the evening ended, I nodded smugly in agreement and then skimmed ahead of my back-thumping friend into the nicotine queen's wake.

And then I stopped.

Written in lipstick across a mirrored lobby wall beside a reflection of my own wrinkled nose I saw nine words: *There, but for the grace of God, go I!*

Were the words the product of my imagination? I was not sure, but I scurried away to scrub the self-righteous smirk off my face before it froze there.

FOOD FOR THOUGHT

Like our Master said, those who are without sin should throw the first stone.

Sour Gripes

"It's none of my business, of course, but you ought to do something about this house," said the neighbor who had come to borrow our ladder.

Other than that we owned more square feet of stuff than the combined measurements of our closets, I hadn't known the house had problems, but my neighbor pointed to an inch-wide crack between the brick facing and the sidewalk leading to the front door. "This building," he intoned, "is moving away from the sidewalk."

As he shouldered the borrowed ladder and took his gloomy self back down the street, I smiled. The house was not moving away from the sidewalk, of course. After forty-some years of heaven-sent rain, the soil had shifted enough to move the sidewalk from where it once touched the house. Since the front steps began where the sidewalk left off, they, too, had parted company with the brick by maybe a scant half inch.

According to Murphy's Law, "Everything put together falls apart sooner or later." If we lived in that house for another twenty or thirty years, we might eventually need to consider redoing the cement work. Maybe not.

"Thinking negative is not a positive way to live!" I considered shouting after our otherwise good neighbor. I didn't bother, though; I knew that if I'd served him my last half-glass of lemonade, he'd have called the vessel half empty. Gloom 'n' doomers tend to get a mite stubborn and possessive over what some of us might call a bad habit of looking on the black side of every hole.

Like age and tight pajamas, negative notions tend to creep up on a person. Youth tends to see the sunny side of life, but gradually the clouds creep in. The older we get, the cloudier life looks, even at church. One day you cheerfully supported whatever might win folks to the Lord and build them up in Him—and the next day you're gloomily shaking your head thinking, *But it's never been done that way before.*

The bulletin's folded wrong, the building too costly, and the preacher uses (or doesn't use) the NIV. While the congregation goes downhill in a green persimmon basket led by Neil Diamond look-alikes, the young tuck their Jesus-logoed T-shirts into too-short shorts, and the changing face of church literature looks suspiciously unholy. Eventually, we conclude, as we shake our heads in disapproval, that there ain't nothin' in all Christendom gonna turn out right.

Since it takes something like nine positives to clear away the mess left by a single negative, maybe the time has come to revive the old popular tune that said we should accentuate the positive, get clean rid of the negative, and never mess with stuff landing in the cracks.

FOOD FOR THOUGHT

Could be that Robert Frost penned these words just for naysayers:

> *I turned to speak to God*
> *About the world's despair;*
> *But to make matters worse*
> *I found God wasn't there.*

In reality, of course, God, like our little brick house, was right where He'd always been. The sidewalk—or in this case, ourselves—was the only thing that moved.

Cause and Effect

Causes, in my opinion, have become as thick as Iowa chiggers on a hot summer night—and twice as pesky. Our desire to save, preserve, protect, donate, give up, stamp out, and pick up sometimes puts even the Holy Spirit on hold. For some of us, ignoring an urgent "cause" is like removing the tag from a mattress. We simply can't do it.

I got to thinking about all this up at Lake Louise last summer after we'd laced up our grungiest tennies and begun a five-hour hike that turned our legs to jelly and left me with some food for thought. At the start of our climb, we passed what looked like a group of morning "partiers" and paused to gawk at a giant, Swiss-type horn on a stand near the water's edge.

The morning was perfect for hiking, our surroundings

as clean as a new robin's egg—except for one thing. "Why is it," I asked, pointing to a cigarette butt on the path ahead, "that smokers consider themselves exempt from the proper disposal of trash?"

"I don't know," Norm said in his patient, here-we-go-again tone.

Well, somebody needed to care! I decided then and there to make this my cause for the day.

Ten butts later, after my mouth had started to feel like a prune that wouldn't let go of its pit, we started up a dirt trail lined with wildflowers. Then I saw another stump of a cigarette, resting this time atop a clump of dewy buttercups. Now my fillings hurt.

The trail grew steeper and rockier. Norm began to puff and I to huff as we came across still another butt lodged among the stones lining a rushing stream. An avalanche crashed in the distance. Norm stood and listened while I filled his other ear on the subject of you-know-what.

We had paused on a rocky ledge to rest when we heard another sound, faint at first, then stronger. "They're playing a hymn," Norm said.

As we listened to the familiar notes of "Amazing Grace," we decided that those we had thought to be partying were instead celebrating what I had temporarily forgotten. The clarion call of that giant Swiss instrument reminded me that while hunting cigarette butts might serve as an exercise for one's righteous indignation, it does nothing to further the cause to which I've long been committed—God's grace.

My focus lifted as we dined on homemade bread with honey near the foot of the glacier before beginning our descent. By the time we'd stumbled back to the business end of Lake Louise, I regretted having wasted so much energy grousing over a lost cause.

When we got home, I sat down to spend some time thanking the Lord for all I'd learned on the journey. Then I called a friend to see what had happened for the cause of Christ while I'd been focusing my attention elsewhere.

FOOD FOR THOUGHT

If you spend all your time trying to remodel the world to your liking, you may never get around to building the Kingdom of God.

Salt Scoop

It has been said that if every volunteer were laid end-to-end, the resulting earth rings would rival those surrounding planet Saturn.

I don't think so.

In the first place, volunteers do not happen in chain-link sequence. They come one at a time and seldom in sufficient quantities. Furthermore, a true volunteer is not likely to get caught lying down, not even for an Associated Press photo or to pad a statistic.

My friend Jane serves as a volunteer at our local hospital, and we have a lot in common—namely three grandchildren and the offspring who first turned the two of us into mothers-in-law. We also belong to the same church, share similar views, and would die in tandem for mere morsels of a two-crust pie. While Jane is the one who volunteers and not I, I know for a fact that if there is globe-circling to be done, she would choose not to recline but to walk.

Assisting patients with menu choices in a high-rise hospital takes more than a little footwork. "Not all volunteer work involves walking," she is quick to explain. "Some tasks are sit-down. Almost anyone can handle those kind."

Well, apparently the tasks are endless. Since chores that fall to volunteers seldom require expertise, even we who are over sixty could handle a few hours a week were it not for our mental habits:

- Me and my comfort first.
- Who wants to get out of a chair and go anyplace?
- I've never done anything like that before.
- I'd probably make a mess of things.
- I'm all out of the habit.
- I can't.
- Let somebody younger than me do it.
- I've had my turn.
- And the classic: Who, me? I don't even know those people.

Early on, Jane began her habit of freeing busy professionals from small and time-consuming chores by joining Pink Ladies and sitting behind a Red Cross information desk. She has since poured gallons of coffee and cold drinks, delivered flowers and mail, set tables, dished out buffet meals, and—you name it!

Somehow all my buts and becauses turn to stubble when I recall that while her husband lay ill with Parkinson's disease, Jane hired a caregiver on hospital days and continued handing out menus.

"At the hospital, I would always see someone who was worse off than we were. Then I'd go home feeling thankful," she says.

Later on, that same plucky spirit helped her to realize that the pain of losing her lifetime companion could be eased through service to others.

Sunday mornings, while most of the older folks were either out to breakfast, still in the shower, or deciding whether or not to lasso their necks for a couple of hours with buttons and ties, Jane was already off to a nursing home. Well into her seventies and no bigger than the salt shaker she represents, she set up chairs, wheeled patients, and cared for their needs while other volunteers conducted morning worship. Now in her eighties, at church Jane treks downstairs on Sunday mornings to help a busy preschool teacher who has but two hands and a whole lot of demands.

When the folks who run the hospital decided the time had come to affirm the work of their many volunteers, Jane, with her seventeen years of service, was the first recipient. The morning she was to be honored, Norm and I donned our glad rags, drove over to the reception, and found Jane wearing her clay pink volunteer's jacket as usual. It would soon be time for lunch trays to go out, but an entire kitchen staff showed up with grateful hugs.

As the reception crowd dwindled, Jane glanced at the clock, then looked at the reception table. "I'll get to work on this mess as soon as folks clear out."

"Jane, not after your own party," I protested.

She picked up the punch bowl. "I don't know why not."

FOOD FOR THOUGHT

Like most volunteers, Jane does not serve to be recognized, but to quietly sprinkle the salt of Christ over those who need it. Embarrassed over so much attention, when a friend said he'd seen her name on the hospital marquee, she quipped, "Oh, that? I think that must be the 'most wanted' list."

It could be Jane is right. She is exactly the sort of person the Kingdom of God most wants.

Put Up or Shut Up

George Burns was wrong when he said, "It's too bad that all the people who know how to run the country are busy driving taxicabs and cutting hair."

While I've never traded first names with a cabbie or been driven much of anyplace by one, I know for a fact that running the country is not a part of the job description for the nice girl who cuts my hair. She mostly runs water and hair dryers.

Furthermore, if it's mere words we're discussing (i.e., air-powered know-how), there are those among my peers who could run the country, the church, and our entire school system single-lipped. Listen near election time, though, and you soon learn that many of the same would never think of doing away with lip service long enough to go register opinion on the business side of a ballot.

An old Chinese proverb says, "When the teeth fall out, the tongue wags loose." I know this to be true because no other group on our side of the planet has more to say on subjects dealing with what ought and ought not to be than we who are over sixty. Give us a topic—say politics or religion, raunchy television, raising kids, or even what ails the president's dog—and the combined clamor of our denture-clad mouths turns into a murmuration equal to ground run-off in a Midwestern downpour.

The truth is, this fastest growing segment of our population is all talk. And talk (due to natural laws that govern supply and demand) is cheap. Maybe that's why so many of us can afford to double-tithe opinion and give so liberally unto others such overpowering doses of what no longer applies to ourselves.

I recently came across a scary bit of wisdom from the pen of nineteenth-century cracker-barrel philosopher, Henry Wheeler Shaw, better known as Josh Billings. "As men grow older," he wrote, "their opinions, like their diseases, grow chronic." While I don't know this for a fact, I suspect that were Josh around to philosophize today, he would also include women in such a statement.

That word "chronic" suggests habits resistant to all

81

efforts toward eradication; its use should prod at least a few of us gray heads into behavior more edifying than what goes on at the usual senior center and church social brouhaha. Understanding that "chronic" can also be applied to a calloused indifference toward moral rot ought to frighten the Geritol out of all but the most atrophied of us. It should jerk us up out of our recliners and prod the more agile among prattlers and park bench pontificators into the simple exercise of standing up for what's right, at least long enough to be counted—even if we have to lean on a cane to do it!

Might be some of us could fold brochures. Or (here's a daring thought) we could invite the ornery kids next door (the ones who planted furrows with their in-line skates among the dahlias) to go to Sunday school. In the backseats of our cars—every Sunday. So they could learn decent values that they could one day stand up for and pass on.

There's an old proverb that suggests no one can till a field by turning it over mentally—or by rolling it off a tongue for that matter. The truth, after all is said and done, is that the words of armchair lecturers accomplish very little. The only way we can change things is when we make the effort to get up off our duffs and move.

FOOD FOR THOUGHT

Along with a whole lot of other "time to's," King Solomon said there is "a time to be silent and a time to speak" (Ecclesiastes 3:7). While good old King Sol may have been the wisest man who ever lived, he should have added one more thing:

There is also a time to put our actions—or our money (or both)—where our mouths are.

Foxed Out

If there's one thing we who are over sixty have had ample years for developing, it's our attitudes. Just the title of Patsy Clairmont's book, *Sportin' a 'Tude,* carries a message guaranteed to get beneath more than one patch of timeworn skin.

We're the folks who've tucked our shirts in, out, and in again; yo-yoed hemlines; gone from easy listening to hard-on-the-hearing music; and made it through one or two world wars. We've observed, considered, ignored, and reacted to the good, the bad, and the ugly for more years than the United Nations.

Renegade attitudes, however, are most often generated not by music or fashion or history but by everyday people and events. As Solomon once said, "[It's] the little foxes that ruin the vineyards" (Song of Songs 2:15).

Right. And what gives me an attitude are the neighbors' camel-sized dogs playing squat tag among my petunias.

Since people are more important than posies, and life is around 10 percent what you make it and 90 percent how you take it, I suppose I could yell quietly at the dogs and smile at the neighbors while soothing my attitude with a definition touted by Elbert Hubbard: "Righteous indignation is your own wrath, as opposed to the shocking bad temper of others." I might, in fact, meet all of my neighborhood problems with tender compassion were it not for our paperboy.

Morning after morning, our newspaper was nowhere to be found and neither was the boy. When I at last got ahold of his ear (verbally and not literally, which is just as well), he nonchalantly asked, "Did you look in the bushes?"

"We've asked you to please put the paper on the porch."

"Well, try looking in the bushes."

On rainy days, we must always "make every effort to live in peace with all men [and one boy] and to be holy" (Hebrews 12:14). Keeping one's attitude in check while peeling wet headlines off Tuesday's grocery ad without tearing "Dear Abby" is not easy. Finding room on our tiled entry floor for all that and an equally soggy sports section is even worse.

Since repeated reminders, laced generously with the word "porch," did no good, after ruminating, contemplating, and deliberating through several such incidents, I finally spoke to his supervisor.

"He's really a good kid," I hastened to insert into my complaint. "Our paper is always on time, and he never forgets to leave one. For one so young, he's quite diligent. Really, I hated to have to say anything; he's such a little guy."

For the next three days, a neatly rolled newspaper landed on our front porch with remarkable accuracy. After congratulating myself for having turned a wayward kid around with kindness rather than frustrated confrontation, I said to Norm, "I think we've finally got ourselves one good paperboy."

A snap judgment, they say, has a way of becoming unfastened.

On the seventh day, after our newspaper had landed on the roof, beside the porch, under the bushes, and out in the rain, while we were still fuming over the damp mess, our granddaughter came to visit.

"The paperboy is such a little guy," I told her. "I hate to be too hard on him, but—"

She raised one doubtful eyebrow. "Isn't his name Joe?"

"Joe Rapscallion. You know him?"

She nodded. "That 'little guy' is in my class." The visiting granddaughter is more than halfway through high school.

FOOD FOR THOUGHT

Since small irritations like Solomon's little foxes
appear more often than the daily newspaper, I'm
going to need to find a cushion to fall back on
that's a whole lot softer than righteous indignation.

Wastepaper

Through more trial than error, Norm and I have developed a foolproof system for keeping our long-term marriage intact while hanging wallpaper: He lifts the ladder from its peg in the garage, carries it in, sets it up, draws me a plumb line, loans me his canvas shop apron, and disappears among the maze and mystery of his beloved garage. I stuff the apron with tools, mount the ladder, and proceed to hang paper. He stays within hearing distance, responds to desperate hollers for help, makes lunch, and orders dinner.

When my friend Lib decided to wallpaper her dining room, however, she insisted that Porter, her thumb-blessed spouse, contribute equal labor to the project. Together, they lugged the ladder, drove to the store for a second shop apron, and argued over the best way to come up with a plumb line.

Lib cut the first strip of paper too short, and Porter forgot to leave a two-inch lap at the corner. The fact that Lib had neglected to buy prepasted wallpaper ensured chaos, and Port's tripping over the paste bucket was indisputably Lib's fault. Still, while no one fixed lunch, he grimly sponged a half gallon of paste from the carpet while Lib mixed more.

By nap time, the two had run out of wallpaper. Lib returned to the store for more but forgot to ask for the same run number. Although Porter's stomach was by now seeking nourishment, he told Lib to keep her T-shirt tucked; he'd write down the number and locate the proper match.

Shortly after 10 P.M., having dined on one leftover cupcake along with peanut butter scrapings smeared over salt-free saltines, Port had had all the wallpapering he could take. He fumed over room dimensions and the size of the task; he belittled Lib's know-how. Then he stalked out to the garage, revved the engine of his blue Dodge pickup, shoved it in and then out of reverse, and headed off down the street.

After Port finally cooled down, he went home. He found that the car had vanished along with Lib. While paste dried in the brushes, he tore open a diet cola and paced. Lib took her sweet time returning to the cottage of their dreams, but eventually she did come back.

Those last few curls of carefully measured, matched wallpaper lay on the floor for weeks, though. Lib and Port eventually patched things up and, to the best of my knowledge, lived happily ever after—but that south wall never did get papered.

Lib and Porter's story reminds me of a church that is threatening to split in two over something just as trivial as wallpaper. In the church's case, however, it happens to be choir robes and a computerized bulletin that are the bones of contention.

Other churches have other hassles to confront. On Sunday mornings, the music may be dull or deafening; building programs may be controversial; youth leaders and pastors may grate on the congregation's nerves; and the air-conditioning may be either too cold or too hot. All these differences are hashed over and gossiped about— but all too seldom are they prayed about and quietly talked over. Forgiveness hits the skids, and the stuff of Matthew 28:19 and Acts 1:8 gets trampled beneath the transient feet of the habitually disgruntled. Friends and neighbors shy away even if they do happen to get invited, which is seldom. Teens and children wander through mixed messages and get lost. Pastors become discouraged and nothing much gets done.

Funny how when we try to accomplish something, division and anger have a knack for getting in our way.

FOOD FOR THOUGHT

Belonging to a church is a little like being married. Despite the sometimes frequent irritations, you just have to find a way to get along. No spouse—and no church—is perfect. But like wallpaper, love covers a multitude of sins.

Mouse Motivation

"I always thought I'd like to go on one of those work and witness trips. I'll never do it now," one new retiree said to another.

"I know what you mean," his friend replied. "I figured when I retired I'd invest in a camper and some paint and go around surprising a few of those small churches that barely squeak by. Well, it's too late now."

I've got news for those two old boys. As J. J. Walker so aptly put it, "If you're there before it's over, you're on time." Believe it or not, I learned that while shopping.

"I can't believe you bought that," Norm said the day I came home from a particular spree wearing a watch I had thought for a long time might be fun to own. He has since periodically repeated himself.

This man who detests shopping also "protects" my claim to sanity by explaining to all who will listen, "It's what happens when your wife goes shopping by herself."

Shopping solo, of course, freed me to sort out my feelings concerning the watch before having to explain my actions to Norm. That I needed a watch was obvious. While the Elgin once given to me by Norm ran fine, its band fittings were obsolete, and we could no longer find replacements to fit them. When the watchband gave out yet again, I decided not to try fixing it. We had long shopped at a store where one could count on outstanding merchandise at great low prices. I would simply buy myself a new watch.

Unfortunately, since it was just weeks past the holidays, stock was low. The few watches left on display in that store were not to my liking. Chin in hands, I folded my elbows across a polished oak counter edge and peered absently through the glass as I pondered my next move.

Since I tend to function better with the time close at hand, being without a watch equaled losing my glasses. Still, I supposed I should remain loyal to our post-holiday budget and the store with the great low prices. . .which meant waiting for a new shipment.

At that very moment (readers with no imagination will not understand nor need they attempt to believe this), a little gold mouse grinned broadly up at me from the face of a watch located smack-dab in the center of the display case—and then the mouse winked. A hovering young clerk on her way to promotion unlocked a sliding glass door, took out the watch, and laid it over my wrist. But while the clown section of my brain recalled bygone yearnings for just such a watch and considered how much fun it would be to wear it, I was also shaking my head.

"I'd feel silly," I said—although down in my heart I knew that I would not.

"These little cartoon characters are no longer just for kids," the girl warbled. "You can wear them at any age."

"Honey, I was born before that mouse ever graced a drawing board," I said.

Her blue eyes widened. "What does that have to do with anything? You're as young as you feel."

The slim leather band on that Mickey Mouse watch goes with my favorite dress and can be tucked beneath a sleeve whenever it doesn't match. My grandkids say my watch is cool. Furthermore, in spite of Norm's teasing, I have never once regretted my purchase, for it marks a new beginning in my approach to life.

From now on, I'm resolved to never say I'm too old to achieve a long-postponed goal. If I can finally wear a

Mickey Mouse watch, at my age, then I can certainly still serve the Lord.

FOOD FOR THOUGHT

For me, the little mouse on my wrist reinforces the words of King Solomon when he said, "There is a time for everything, and a season for every activity under heaven" (Ecclesiastes 3:1). Could be that the season is here, right now.

Folks around us just might benefit if we who are over sixty would stop coddling our regrets. It's about time we got on with whatever it was we thought God was calling us to do in the first place.

Worrywarts

If there was ever an exercise designed for those of us who are older, it's worry. Men, in fact, have actually grown bald during the process of worrying over losing their hair. And, according to Nancy Drew, "If worry were effective as a weight-loss program," we with our paunches and pudding bag profiles might soon "be invisible."

The truth is, while pounds lost by worry have a way of sneaking back, according to Charles Mayo and other good doctors, worry does damage the nervous system as well as hearts and glands and circulation. So why in the name of good health do we aging ones worry?

For one thing, worry is something to do when you can't do a thing about something that's none of your business. You worry about choices made by your grown kids, the grandkids, everybody else's kids, and the wars you're too old to help fight.

What's on TV worries you; presidents, politics, and potholes worry you; and so does the way your neighbor builds his fence.

We fret over what went wrong in the past, what's happening in the present, and what's apt to go awry in the future.

Worry, whether it does any good or not, is one wrong move we who belong to the over-the-hill gang seem to think we're entitled to make. "It goes with the territory," we say—the territory being advancing age. The trouble with worries at any age, however, is that, like babies, they tend to grow bigger when you nurse them.

One thing we who are over sixty no longer have to worry about is what people think of us. By now, most of us have learned it is highly unlikely that people are thinking of us at all. Much of whatever else we perceive as worrisome may fall in the same category. Winston Churchill, in fact, delighted in telling the story of the old man who said on his deathbed that "he had had a lot of trouble in his life, most of which never happened."

One item we Nervous Nellies like to make sure we've attended to is interest. If we do have the means, which some of us do not, we still don't like paying any interest. Interest, we've finally learned, eats principal. And principal is what pays our bills.

Knowing all this, it beats me why any of us would want to worry. Worry, they tell me, is a mighty high rate of interest to be paying in sleepless nights and loss of appetite on troubles that may or may not ever come due.

"Worry," says Mitzi Chandler, "is as useless as a handle on a snowball." What's more, worry zaps away energy, steals time, ruins happiness, wrinkles faces, repeats remorse, freaks out over fears, and sweats the sort of small stuff that's not worth a drop of perspiration. All at the same time,

Worry never climbed a hill,
Worry never paid a bill,
Worry never darned a heel,
Worry never cooked a meal.
It never led a horse to water,
nor ever did a thing it oughter.

Anonymous

Instead, worry agitates like my old washing machine. And like Grandma's rocking chair, it keeps constantly rocking but never gets us anyplace.

FOOD FOR THOUGHT

A long time ago Jesus said we were not to worry about life, food, our bodies, or whatever else might bring on nail biting or draw butterflies to mess with our midsections (Matthew 6:25–34; Luke 12:22–31). He said that worry was a waste of time, because He is more than prepared to meet every need we can dream up to fret over.

The truth is that worry, even at its finest, is never about God or His readiness to bring peace and comfort and solutions. It's about us old worrywarts.

Period.

Face-Lift

While Abraham Lincoln had about the longest face ever to be hung on the schoolroom walls of history, his droll words—"Most folks are about as happy as they make up their minds to be"—are right on.

Though we all know that whatever heredity did for a face can be drastically altered by circumstances, most of us can't use the crushing weight of the Civil War as an excuse for our sourpuss expressions. On the other hand, attitudes in need of adjustment, the daily nursing of discontent, can turn faces into gargoyles that may frighten one's very own mother.

Case in point: We once had elderly neighbors, two sisters, who lived next door in a house surrounded by flowers. The dining room in that house had a fine bay window, through which one or the other or both of the sisters could often be seen observing the comings and goings of our children.

The face of the older sister, the one who tended the flowers, was like a plump ripe fig with lots of wrinkles in all the right places. If she ever stopped smiling, no one else ever knew about it.

Her sister's countenance, on the other hand, was more like the last dried prune in the bag, the cull missed by sorters, the sour, stick-to-the-pit prune true prune-lovers avoid. If that one ever smiled, it must have been some event!

While I haven't a clue as to what turned those sisters into opposites, we could tell by the rhetoric following the rapping on our back door that our children added form to those faces:

"I thought you ought to know. Those kids have been in Effie's flowers again."

"I made cookies. May they have one now? Or should I wait until after they've had lunch?"

"If a kid of mine ever swung on my clothesline, she wouldn't be able to sit down for a week!"

"Please, may I borrow your sweet children for an hour?"

"We used to have a little peace and quiet in this neighborhood."

"I brought the children some snapdragons to play with. See, dears, how they open their mouths like tiny lions when you squeeze them."

No need to say who said what, for as playwright Bertolt Brecht so aptly put it, "What's joy to one is a nightmare to the other." And the stuff from which nightmares are formed is not made in one day. It takes practice to let kids turn you into a real grump.

Some of life's little annoyances tend to mess with the moods of those of us who are over sixty more than others. For instance:

- Slow traffic.
- Fast traffic.
- Late newspapers.
- Your mate's penchant for shopping.
- Your mate's resistance to shopping.
- Change.
- Daybreak racket from any lawn mower other than your own.
- The remote in the hands of another.
- The new preacher.
- The old preacher.
- Teenagers (in general).

- In-laws (specific).
- Temperature.
- Panty hose.
- Neckties.
- And, finally, while the late Charley Schultz considered a "warm puppy" a synonym for "happiness," one person's pet to another's lawn can spell the direct opposite.

The list could go on because we all can name stuff that annoys us. The trick is to hang onto one's own pet list of gripes and, at the same time, keep our pesky little attitudes from reaming disgruntled ditches across our faces.

It can't be done. Might pay to double-check in a mirror now and then.

FOOD FOR THOUGHT

Remember: "A happy heart makes the face cheerful" (Proverbs 15:13). I don't know about you, but as far as I'm concerned, no angry attitude or gripe grist I can think of is worth the price or the pain of a face-lift.

Part 4

PICTURES FROM THE PASTURE

The LORD is my shepherd,
I shall not be in want.
He makes me lie down in green pastures,
he leads me beside quiet waters.
PSALM 23:1–2

Misfits

My husband is one of those happy victims of corporate fallout known as the early retiree. It is now several years later, and on winter mornings I am still getting used to having my eyes jerked open along with the bedroom drapes as he gloats over snow shovelers scurrying to clear their driveways so they can go to work.

What's a retiree doing home between Thanksgiving and Good Friday? Why aren't we lolling on the sands of our fiftieth state? Or checking out Fort Lauderdale?

Peer pressure, that's why. They stared at us in Tucson that first September. True, we were newly retired and had a lot to learn. Still, our being novitiates hardly merited such a roomful of stares. Darkness had already fallen when we had parked our little brown Zephyr in front of our motel the evening before—so how did they know we weren't the proud owners of one of a dozen motor homes dotting the parking area?

As gawkers go, these were a refined group. RVs or no, they had holed up on a Saturday night for regular baths. We all gathered in the lounge of one accord to partake of the "free" Continental breakfast.

Styrofoam cups in hand, Norm and I located a vacant plastic table and sat. "Apricot," I murmured, biting into the portion of my Danish that oozed the most synthetic jam.

A woman wearing a red and white tablecloth-check blouse turned and peered at me. As her curious stare slithered over to Norm, I scanned my bosom for possible spills.

"I know," I said, lowering my voice. "It's because we're the only ones dressed for church."

But Norm's three-piece suit was home in the closet, his shirt open-throat. And there was nothing showy about my shirtwaist dress.

Tired of playing early-morning wide screen for the entertainment of the other guests, Norm polished off his wilted Bismark and asked, "Are we about ready to go?"

Never one to walk away from a puzzle still minus its last piece, I said, "Not quite." Before I left, I needed to figure out why our appearance was drawing all these stares.

Swallowing the last of my lukewarm coffee, I swiveled my head. One trip around the circle and I knew what made us different: Without exception, each of the other couples was dressed alike! Both tablecloth top and her partner had on red socks and navy blue slacks, and his shirt was an oversized twin to hers. Another pair wore serviceable brown polyester, while yet another was attired in wrinkled khaki shorts and jungle-print shirts. I guessed that the trim couple in blue and white held joint ownership to a boat and motor home in the same crisp colors parked outside.

Being new to the off-season road and mere babes, how were we to know? We don't even own wedding bands alike. Not to worry, though. Cash in the IRAs and we, too, could register at the Super 8 dressed in tandem.

We should never have suggested it to our daughter. She doesn't care if every geriatric in Sun City is doing it; we cannot. As she points out, our skins don't match.

Thinking back, a whole lot more than our outfits were out of sync in Tucson that morning. Although we had dressed as usual and on purpose for worship, perhaps no one else in that room understood this was the Lord's Day. The scenario repeats wherever we travel: We meet a few who gladly recognize our Maker, but far more do not. Outward appearances seem more important than eternal concerns.

FOOD FOR THOUGHT

We now have matching sweatshirts bearing the handprints of three of our grandsons. Our compliance to the duo-dressing rule, however, does nothing to alter the mind-set of our fellow retirees toward Christ.

We may have to open our mouths and allow the Lord to fill them with something other than jelly donuts.

Fringe Benefits

Someone has said that there is peace in any home where folks keep themselves scattered and seldom make the mistake of trying to get together.

Considering the years my lifelong partner spent flying the friendly skies and jouncing over back country roads while I stayed home and kept the word processor and everything else running, one could truthfully say we've been there, done that, past tense, thank You, Lord.

Shortly before my spouse turned in his company pass, a friend suggested that marital adjustment was not listed among the incentives that come with early retirement. "What kind of life can you possibly have with him under your tennies all day?" she asked.

For starters, I knew beyond question that God had not

only ordained marriage, but He had also showered Norm and me with joyful serendipity along the way. For Him to yank the rug of wedded bliss from beneath us now that we finally had more time for all the other surprises He had up His sleeve didn't make sense.

"My daily routine is bound to go better if I've got someone to talk to," I insisted. Then I dusted off an old cliché, which may have come from Bombeck: "I married him for life, not for lunch."

Next, a neighbor whose spouse had retired complained, "Yesterday he asked me to go with him to the gas station. Why would I want to go with him or anyone else just to buy gas?"

While I usually find that going almost anyplace with Norm is pretty nice, I didn't want to argue. In tones as flat as a skid mark, I said, "Wow," and let the word fizzle off onto the period before suggesting, "Surely you venture sometimes beyond Chevron City?"

"Yes," my neighbor answered, "and I'm supposed to be thrilled with visiting some out-of-the-way place I've never once thought about wanting to see."

I'm going to love that part! almost popped off my tongue before I could smother the words beneath a ripple of soothing laughter. "Honey, don't you know men design

111

side jaunts so they won't have to learn enough French to take us to Paris?"

"Give him a week, and he'll have his fist welded to the remote," whined another dowager seated beside me at a retiree forum. "I haven't chosen a channel since my man quit working and planted petunias in his dinner bucket."

Television being low on my list of ways to spend time, I let that one pass. However, now that Job's comforters had planted their negatives, some of the worst flack came from within. I had my own set of internal skeptics:

"You'll be running around when you'd rather be writing," they said.
And be stumbling on fresh grist for whenever I can write, I answered.

"You'll be stopping mid-muse to smear peanut butter sandwiches for his lunch," they whined.
And have someone to smear sandwiches for me when a deadline is looming, I reassured the skeptics.

"Your chores will increase," they warned.
To quote an old Vermont proverb, I responded, *It's a*

lonesome washing when there's not a man's shirt in the load.

Now, having had plenty of time to decide whether I'm for or against having my best friend underfoot, I'm convinced that the truth about retired life has somehow been hidden along with good mothers-in-law and some of life's other best-kept secrets. I like being with my husband. That's why I married him in the first place.

FOOD FOR THOUGHT

Martin Luther was right: "There is no more lovely, friendly or charming relationship, communion or company, than a good marriage"—particularly when it's been blessed with time in which to grow.

Midsummer Life's Scheme

Telephone advertising is out to shovel me under. The pitch goes something like this:

"Hello, my name is Fritzie. We're all going to die someday, right?"

And with that opener, Fritzie is off, trying to sell me a funeral plan offering snug-in benefits vastly beyond the "final rest" options selected by any of our other over-sixty friends.

But before interment comes retirement, right? Can't people allow us to enjoy where we're at right now before shoving us along to the next stage?

I have to admit, of course, that our plans for our leisure years did in fact begin early as well. Long before we retired, we senior citizens joined savings plans, collected road maps, and dreamed of endless fishing and knitting and propping of feet. Sometimes we even reveled in the possibility of having more time to serve others. As we faced our retirement years, though, what we didn't like to think about was those precasket years when our hands would grow too gnarled to knit and a day's work might consist of lifting a foot to prop. We'd much prefer to live lazily for years, and then, if necessary, fade for a few days in a nursing home before jetting quietly off to heaven. In our minds, there are no what-ifs, no alternative plans for anything less than the ideal.

Unfortunately, this sort of mind-set fails to notice that turning up one's nose at senior meals or opting to suffer it out on the old family farm can become an ordeal for loved ones and a nightmare for caregivers. It's not easy attending to the needs of elderly neighbors or loved ones, dealing with their health and safety, hunger and mobility, medications and the disrepair of their surroundings. Cross-country, out-of-town loved ones make the whole process harder.

We who are over sixty need to consider winter while we're still enjoying the summer of life. We need to explore options and answer questions before our kids and the paramedics get to have all the say.

For instance, if I should opt to remain in my present

home no matter what, is it a suitable place in which to grow old? Will funds be available for my care and my home's eventual upkeep? Who will I depend on to run errands? For daily care? Are my loved ones aware of my expectations? How close are health facilities? Is my neighborhood safe? What are the options for obtaining balanced meals? Who will make decisions if and when (heaven forbid) I cannot?

Now that more folks are living long enough to become dependent on their children, retirement homes—where your toenails get trimmed and a dispenser of pills comes regularly to your door—are mushrooming. If health and safety and freedom from dust mops and hedge clippers are important, this option is well worth exploring.

While apartment living or a smaller home may work for some, anyone who intends to simply move in with the kids needs to answer these questions:

- Do the kids know your plans?
- Is your presence okay with the one who married your offspring?
- Are you sure?

These questions are real sticklers—but you better be sure you know the answers.

Helping out a little bit with the needs of older folks within our circle has left Norm and me with a truckload of food for thought. While we can still (with a bit of puffing) hike up a hill, when we built our small retirement home, we opted for no stairs, easy faucets, and a sit-down spot in the shower. What's more, when the time comes for me to resign from housework, I will gladly call up those Merry Maids. And what woman doesn't long at times for someone else to do the cooking? While the mind-set of some we know remains just that—set—we thought we'd made a great start toward planning wisely for those later-on years for ourselves.

Then, following a particularly trying week of looking after oldsters no longer able to look after themselves, I had to go and blab to our daughter: "When I get old and refuse help with pills—or whatever simply must be done—will you please make me do it anyhow?"

She handed me a piece of paper. "Can I get that in writing?"

I wrote it.

She pointed. "Now sign it."

FOOD FOR THOUGHT

Whatever any of us decide about the future, we would do well to keep in mind this fact: "Many are the plans in a man's heart, but it is the LORD's purpose that prevails" (Proverbs 19:21). If we, "commit to the LORD whatever you do" (Proverbs 16:3), our plans will not only succeed; they will probably turn out to be what is truly best for us.

Freewheelin'

If Anais Nin was right and "Life shrinks or expands according to one's courage," then the day we bought the fifth wheel is also the day I moved to Lilliput.

Having no desire to sail down even the broadest of freeways towing fifty-five hundred pounds of aluminum-shrouded stuff, I warned Norm, "You'll have to do the driving."

Evidently, several months of squatting to examine RV underpinnings had tipped reality to the far end of Norm's thinking. "No problem," he said.

"What if you get sleepy?" I risked suggesting to a man who has racked up thousands of accident-free miles.

"If I'm tired," he assured me, "we'll stop."

And he was true to his word. During those first few

trips with the fifth wheel, he never once nodded off—and I only occasionally jabbed myself with the business end of a counted cross-stitch needle.

The pricks to my conscience were something else. I hated the high, clumsy feel of the dumb pickup, but that was no excuse for not taking my usual turns at the wheel.

We traded the old truck for a smoother-riding pickup, and still I could not bring myself to head down a highway pulling what in my mind had become a land monster. While I took yet another passenger-seat guilt trip, my life's partner drove every paved inch of our longest trip ever.

Fear is like that. Even those of us who are old enough to know better can find plenty of "what ifs" that can scare us into shopping for gravesites. We lump fears as diverse as flying and trips to the dentist into one category—dying. We fear change, future illness, and the diminishing of our skills.

Martin Luther King once said, "Courage faces fear and thereby masters it." Besides, I reminded myself one day as we were rolling along a stretch of all-but-deserted freeway, *whatever became of trust?* I once taught kids, "Be strong and courageous. Do not be terrified; do not be discouraged, for the LORD your God will be with you wherever you go" (Joshua 1:9). Had I already forgotten that often-repeated Sunday school lesson?

My side-view mirror told me the RV was still behind me. So were a lot of other things, I realized—fearsome obstacles for which I had claimed the promise of that very verse:

. . .the panic that struck prior to public speaking and
    before all six root canals;
    . . .fears accompanying a child's illness;
        . . .unwanted moves;
           . . .spiders in my bedroom;
             . . .and so much more.

God had been with me through them all.

I was reminded of the first time I turned into a quivering chicken at the thought of flying alone; that time God sent, not angels, but four world-traveled missionaries who surrounded me with fascinating tales and got me where I needed to be.

Now the wide rolling roads of Wyoming lay ahead, while beside me sat a man who demonstrates more patience in a single day than I can hope to claim in a lifetime. "If you want me to," I quavered, "I think I could try driving—"

He instructed me, talked me through the tough places, and drove all the difficult roads himself. When we pulled into my mother-in-law's driveway two days later, the fifth wheel was still behind me, as were a few more of my fears

We were on our way home, when a tight-lipped woman driving an eighteen-wheeler began hogging more than her share of a Montana four-lane. Mentally whipping out my verse, I white-knuckled my way through that and several more situations before I finally relaxed. Southbound from Spokane, Norm fell asleep, and I was on my own—but not really. God's promise was still with me.

When we got home, however, I surrendered the wheel and watched while Norm backed the fifth wheel through the gate and onto its pad between our fence and the neighbor's. When God promised I would never need to be afraid, I don't figure He meant me to abandon all common sense. After all, we all have very real human limitations. And maneuvering the RV in reverse is one of mine.

FOOD FOR THOUGHT

True, God promised I need never be afraid. And we can depend on God's Word. But we'd better be pretty clear He really directed us before we leap off a tall building, stop taking our medication, or risk our safety in some other reckless way. Even acting on a promise of God demands good sense.

Yes, Virgil,
There Is a Savior

Dear Editor:

I am sixty years old. Some of my retired friends tell me that Christmas is a crock of ancient Palestinian baloney; that while Jesus may well have been born in a cow stable, a God who can change lives does not exist. My old Christian Daddy said, "If you see it in the Holy Book, it's so." Please, Sir, deliver me no guff; is there a Savior?

Virgil O'Hankerin'
In Sun City Somewhere

Virgil, your pals are wrong. They have been brainwashed by the selfishness of a me-centered age. They only believe what they see on the evening news. They think that nothing exists save that which they've dreamed up on their own. Closed minds, Virgil, be they sheltered by hair or mere skin, tend to shrink.

Yes, Virgil, there is a Savior named Jesus. Because He lives, we can know the certainty of peace and joy and unconditional love and can live productive lives filled with goodness and purpose and beauty. Minus a Savior, our world would be a sorry place in which to live. There would be no one in whom to have faith, no songs in the night, no reason to pray, no hope. The Christmas season might still be filled with trees and tinsel, but there would be no sense of wonder or awe. The Light of the World would be extinguished.

Not believe in the Savior! You might as well not believe in electricity. You might hire private detectives to infiltrate churches and shadow all those who call themselves Christians, but even if you never once caught a single glimpse of the Savior, what would that prove? Nobody sees our Savior in a body these days, but that doesn't mean there is no Savior.

His presence in a life is the most real thing in the world, and that is something neither you nor I can see. Did you ever see your voice float over a thousand miles as you talked with a friend on your phone? Of course not, but that's no proof that your voice was not there. Nobody can conceive or imagine all the wonders God has wrought through the lives of people committed to Him.

No Savior? Thank God He lives, and He lives forever. A billion years from now, Virgil, yes, ten thousand times ten trillion years from now, though this world will pass away, He will reign forever and continue to make glad the hearts of all.

FOOD FOR THOUGHT

All of us benefit from modern inventions like electricity and the telephone—but how many of us really understand how these things function? By the same token, there is a mystery covering spiritual matters that not even the best electrical engineer or wisest philosopher can penetrate. Only through childlike faith in the Son of God can we see beyond the veil that was torn in two when He died on the Cross; only through Jesus can we glimpse the awesome miracle of His resurrection and one day share in His glory. In all the world, there is nothing else that is real and abiding.

Retreat at Epicure Gorge

"You can't beat a retreat for helping a new believer get his feet on the ground," I said to our friend Mackenzie last Sunday as our organist crescendoed through "We'll Work Till Jesus Comes."

Our newly converted pew mate opened his bulletin and glanced at the announcements. "Oh, really?" he whispered.

I was about to elaborate when an usher paused with plate in hand. Clutching my bag where my spare change lay hidden, I passed the plate on to Mackenzie, who dropped in a tithe envelope.

"It costs two hundred bucks," I warned. Then I added, "We've yet to attend a retreat that wasn't worth every cent."

The choir sang and then came the sermon. Impatiently, I waited until after church to finish telling Mackenzie about the adult retreat at Old Baldy Inn.

"Or, if you're into prayer, you may prefer to sign up for that five-day seminar at Golf Gulch. We pay, play, and pray—in that order."

Mackenzie's eyebrows came together and knitted a stitch over his nose.

"Excellence is the standard, you understand. And the place does have to make money," I explained.

"Which will you be attending?" Mackenzie asked politely.

"We wouldn't miss either one."

As we talked, my friend Betty sashayed across the foyer and eyeballed me. Finally, I quit conversing with Mackenzie and asked Betty if she wanted something.

"One of our greeters is having surgery next month," she informed me. "Could you substitute on the second Sunday?"

I flipped through my appointment book. "Sorry," I said. "Norm and I are due at the Wills and Trusts Symposium."

"At Dollar Mountain Lodge? Didn't you go last year? And the year before that?"

Thinking it wouldn't hurt for Betty to notice how I was doing right by our new convert, I said, "Mackenzie, there's another retreat for you. A bit more spendy, but—"

Betty interrupted. "Would you be interested in repeating what you said about the Win Some Week Getaway for my Sunday school class? Those ideas for sharing Christ with one's neighbors should fit right in with next week's lesson."

I shook my head. "I really can't afford to miss that confab on compassion."

"That's next Sunday?"

"Starts Friday night. Mackenzie, you should come, too."

"How much?"

"Two-fifty plus food and transportation. The restaurants are first class."

"I'll have to think about it."

"What do you mean you'll have to think about it? I'm telling it to you straight, Mackenzie. If your greatest aim in life is to serve Jesus—"

The pastor tapped my shoulder. "Remember that homeless fellow they arrested in front of the church for vagrancy? He's also been charged with family desertion. Perhaps if you and Norm were to—"

"Reverend," I said, "Norm and I have forms to fill out. The Lost Hills Power Powwow lasts for three days and then there's Dare to Disciple. Mackenzie, do you own an RV? Cathedral Campers is coming up next month. We haven't missed that little baby in nine years. . . .

"Hey, Mackenzie! You're not leaving, are you? Tell me, what could be more important than you and your wife signing up with us for a little spiritual feasting?"

Mackenzie's eyebrows unraveled. "We've got soup cans to box up and send to Mozambique."

"You can't be serious, my friend. This may be news to you—but a Christian's got to be spiritually fed if he wants to grow."

"I always get sick at smorgasbords," Mackenzie said. He turned to the pastor. "What did you say that inmate's name was?"

A new babe in Christ was withering before my eyes! "Mackenzie! You don't owe that jailbird a thing!"

Mackenzie looked me in the eye. "Don't I owe the gospel in the same measure as I have received it?"

FOOD FOR THOUGHT

Getting away is all well and good in its place—
but remember, Jesus does not call us to *retreat;*
instead, He asks us to *advance* the cause of His
kingdom.

Part 5

DOLLARS AND DOODADS

Cast but a glance at riches,
and they are gone,
for they will surely sprout wings
and fly off to the sky like an eagle.
PROVERBS 23:5

R Toys Us?

Yesterday, while browsing through one of those kitchen stores, I picked up a plastic gimmick, pressed a button on one side, and out popped four tiny hooked wires. Adjusting my bifocals, I read the label and thought of all the years I'd speared, stabbed, or finger-wrestled dills from a jar when I might just as well have had a pickle-plucker.

Finding that pickle-plucker started me thinking about gadgets. At bedtime, I closed the utility room door to the muffled hum of the air exchanger, turned off two ceiling fans, and flipped the wire on the ice maker to keep it from going plop in the night. Then I plugged in the motorized water tool recommended by my dentist and flushed the remains of a microwaved dinner from between my teeth. After adjusting the controls on the electric blanket, I said a quick prayer:

Now I lay me down to sleep,
Please, Lord, You know such toys aren't cheap.
If one should quit, please have the grace
To give me two to take its place.

Since our home is replete with doodads that take up space, zap away time, minimize movement, keep us awake, make extra work, and lower the bank balance, I don't know why I prayed that last line.

Furthermore, gizmos tend to wear out, crack, break, squeak, rattle, fizzle, and smoke. And while the average man's stuff tends to be bigger, noisier, and dirtier than the frills that pleasure ladies, sooner or later almost all the "toys" belonging to both genders will lie idle, gather dust, or become obsolete.

What can you do with six assorted cassette players, for instance, now that we've got CDs? And who would have ever thought kids would finger my portable typewriter and ask, "What's that?" And we never dreamed that adequate outlets and the craze for cordless would hit at the same time.

In this age of ownership and display, people think

nothing of tackling a Saturday sale crowd to take home a Swiss, Dutch, or Icelandic waffle cooker—and then buy their waffles frozen.

We buy strange contraptions from kitchen stores and trade our dollars for doohickeys in home centers and auto accessory places. We own boats, RVs, and water, snow, trail, beach, and dune toys; we fill our garage with enough power tools to construct a skyscraper; and we run out of stalls for parking our two or more autos.

A rich young man once got his three-car garage so crammed with widgets he had to tear it down and build space for five. His walk-in closet became more like squeeze-in, and the entire property began to vibrate with the hum of a thousand contraptions. At the same time he got to wondering how much it was going to cost him to buy into eternal life.

Jesus told him it's not true that the man who dies with the most toys wins. The Lord said the gates of heaven had not been designed to accommodate Kenworth tractors pulling dual semi-trailers. He explained to the young man that church ministries geared to compassion had been organized with large donations in mind, and that the Salvation Army and other such charities could easily handle any financial surprise. In short, it's better to give than to accumulate.

FOOD FOR THOUGHT

I don't know about you, but I've never sensed any heavenly opposition to comfort or clever inventions. I suspect there were times when Jesus could have used a vibrating recliner Himself. The rub comes not with ownership but with trading tithes for trinkets, compassion for cash benefits, and a lack of willingness to part with the whole shebang.

Likely, come Judgment Day, we'll all have to drop our toy boxes off at the great yard sale in the sky.

Pleasantville Pursuit

All of us dream of getting something for nothing. I have to confess I've licked my share of envelopes addressed to Publisher's Clearinghouse.

While waiting hopefully one morning for the armored car to arrive from New York bearing my prize money, I noticed our neighbor's two little girls scampering across the street swinging empty red sand pails. A short time later, the doorbell rang.

Lifting her now-full pail for me to see, one asked, "Do you want to buy a beautiful rock that was growed by the ocean?"

"For five cents," the other one added.

Amused, yet disturbed to have caught such young children in the age-old game of something-for-nothing, I said, "They look very much like those over by our driveway. Do you suppose ours also grew beside the ocean?"

The older girl's face reddened. "They didn't really come from the ocean," she said. "We're just pretending."

I could have gone along with their little game, purchased a rock, and been done with it. But I've dealt with children far too long to not feel responsible for their moral development.

Besides, she wasn't smiling. "They're really your rocks," she confessed.

"I know, and we like our rocks," I said. "You may play with them for as long as you like, but please, don't sell them."

Maybe I overreacted. I don't think so. Could be the sting of our having been so recently bilked out of a large sum of money was still with me. Had the friend with whom we'd so trustingly invested begun his dishonest business practices by selling rocks from a neighbor's driveway?

In retrospect, I'll admit that the promised return sounded preposterous. Still, we were gullible (greedy?) enough to sign on the dotted line. Like others caught in the pinch of an outright scam, we were simply seeking added security for our retirement years. Right?

The truth is, while the Bible clearly warns to "Keep

your lives free from the love of money and be content with what you have" (Hebrews 13:5), most anyone would turn five shades of tickled pink to be named by Ed McMahon on the evening news.

Weeks before Norm retired, a covey of moneychangers began hovering near his desk. Evenings, they phoned him at home. At noon, they bought him lunch. While we exercised caution and listened warily to the diamond talk and other investment gossip, in the end, we lost our good sense.

That wasn't all we lost. God's incredible sense of humor, however, came through. While sweepstakes came and sweepstakes went, He saw to it that we got enough post-retirement work to replace every penny of what we'd lost.

I've wondered sometimes if Jesus' homespun garment had pockets, and if so, what might He have carried in them. M & M candies for the kids? For sure, His billfold never bore the bulge of a billion-dollar windfall.

I wonder, too, how fat my wallet would be if I hadn't licked so many stamps for mail addressed to Pleasantville?

FOOD FOR THOUGHT

Even those of us who are inexperienced can avoid financial trouble by following these tips:

- If a deal sounds too good to be true, it probably is.
- Beware of fakes. Know every wart on the nose of your bank representative.
- Consider junk mail junk.
- Never invest money you cannot afford to lose or that is needed for living expenses.
- Ignore both telephone and mail schemes that call for money—namely your money.
- Investing with a friend or relative is seldom wise.
- Deal with familiar businesses and with people you know. Remember, the BBB is not a pop gun for kids. The Better Business Bureau is there to help you, and it's as close as your telephone.
- Doing financial business by cellular or portable phone is a no-no.
- Like the proverbial eggs in one basket, it is generally safer not to invest all your funds in one place.
- Money invested for God brings the greatest return.

Christmas Thrift

It takes a lot of tissue and glitz to wrap Christmas gifts for a family the size of ours. When our girls were small, sometimes we barely got the paper peeled off the last stick-on bow and ourselves into bed before the whisper of fluffy slippers announced it was time to unwrap.

Since our daughters all married and multiplied, wrapping has increased until it has now reached an all-time high. Not to worry. We have it well in hand. Norm wraps all presents equipped with right-angle corners while I tie bows and wrestle with what's left. Further, we no longer wait until past bedtime on Christmas Eve to start.

Still, when I witness the crumpling of all that beautiful paper on Christmas morning, I might as well be hearing fingernails on a chalkboard. Such waste makes every thrifty hair on my head stand on end.

"Please—save the bows!" I beg as a tangle of red satin hits the garbage bag.

When they start stomping perfectly good boxes, I say in my best Depression-child voice, "When I was a kid, we saved all our wrap—ironed it sometimes—kept it in a cardboard dress box to be used again. If we had ribbon at all—"

A teenage upstart interrupts. "Was that back when you walked a kazillion miles to school?" While I am trying to decide if he is kidding, his tone changes. "What kinds of stuff did you get in your wrinkly little packages?"

He couldn't have related if I'd told him, so I simply said, "Let's start with my stocking." I'd just seen a giant Hershey candy bar, CD, a ten-dollar bill, and more spewing from his.

Surrounded suddenly by a great cloud of little and big witnesses, I began my tale. "When we got home from church on Christmas Eve—"

"I thought your folks didn't go to church."

"They didn't. But like everyone else in town, they went to the Christmas program. Their kids were in it."

"Even if they didn't go to church?"

Kids reared on musicals, multi-mikes, and spotlights weren't going to grasp this one either. "Look. In our town, if you even hoped to spell 'Merry Christmas!' in big letters across a platform, you grabbed every kid. But back to my stocking.

"The minute we got home, I would peel off one long brown-ribbed stocking, grab a clothespin from the kitchen clothesline—"

"You hung up a dirty sock? Yuk!"

They had heard my "olden days" laundry lecture before, usually right after they had demanded the immediate cleansing and drying of a favorite T-shirt. I stuck to the subject.

"I always knew what I would get: a big Red Delicious apple from Washington State, one orange, and the exact same number of mixed nuts and chocolate drops as my brothers and sisters."

A slight pause. "That's all?"

Later, after the door had slammed behind kids trying out new in-line skates, I got to thinking. Our grandkids had known almost from the start that wrappings and stocking loot had nothing to do with Jesus. They understood that the real Gift of Christmas had come wrapped in swaddling clothes.

Unlike me, not one of them had ever stood before a crowded church and recited "C is for the Christ Child" without having a clue as to who they were talking about. Most knew Luke 2 well enough to rattle it off before Grandpa could get his Bible open on Christmas morning.

Still, there was no need to be wasteful, I decided as I thanked God for the Unspeakable Gift that had made such a difference in our family.

My perspective shifted from glitz back to grandkids as an ornery son-in-law deposited a neatly tied garbage bag beside my chair. "Sorry about the wrinkles," he said. "Maybe when your time comes to go, these handle ties will make this wad of glitz easier to take with you."

"Thanks," I said. "But when their time comes to go, if it's all the same to you, I'd just as soon save a little corner of heaven for the grandkids."

FOOD FOR THOUGHT

Self-righteousness comes disguised in all sorts of shapes and sizes. If our eyes are fixed on Christ, we'll have little time for either condemning others or patting ourselves on the back.

Dust—Thou Art

If it is true that one's home is a reflection of oneself, then my house proves that God really did fashion human beings from dust.

Recently, while I tried to prepare for an open house, I pondered the dust in the nooks and crannies of my house. I muttered a hastily adapted version of a familiar prayer:

God grant me the gall to tastefully arrange decor over those spots I have no time to clean; the energy to polish whatever I can; and enough memory to recall that white gloves are currently out of fashion.

Back when I still wore hair ribbons, we sometimes

gathered around our battery-operated Philco radio and listened to *One Man's Family*. Punctuated by a steady stream of tea trays and elaborate dinner parties, the lives of this all-adult family hummed endlessly on inside a four-story home that was complete with dust-free heirloom furnishings. That house, including Hattie, was once my dream home.

Hattie kept all four stories spotless while she ironed countless starched white shirts for three generations of men who often discussed money but seldom referred to the business of earning it. Hattie dealt with food and dinner parties, laid tea trays to perfection, hemmed ball gowns, offered sage advice to the young and foolish (more often than not after midnight), and still found time to serve as soloist for the Easter sunrise service. I *know* she could have handled my open house.

The four-story house and the tea trays I could do without, but as the days before my open house dwindled, I desperately needed a Hattie. Hattie, I knew, could have dealt impartially with my clutter.

Norm's photography magazines and crossword paraphernalia, for instance, were a part of his scenic backdrop (as well as his front and side drops). How much could I remove without disturbing the essence of this man who has so cheerfully financed my book buying for going on fifty years? Too cheerfully, perhaps, for some of the oldest volumes had suddenly become a part of the clutter.

But how could I allow such thoughts when many of the most tattered books were also cherished friends? I could no more hide them away in a closet than I could scour away the marks left by my grandkids on my worn kitchen floor.

While trying to bring order out of chaos and become a person I was not in order to impress people who had already accepted me as I am, I experienced the gentle nudge of a still, small Voice asking, *Just what is the big deal here?* Had I not been content with my home as it was? Did my house really need to be anything other than its usual cozy state?

The big event came and went—and I sensed that God was pleased with the whole affair. After the dust settled, it occurred to me that the best was yet to come.

I had fought a good fight with both dust and discontent. My clutter was safe. I had finished my turn. And now I got to go to someone else's open house. Hattie or no Hattie, I meekly promised to be content with my genuine state.

FOOD FOR THOUGHT

Contentment comes not from striving to clone ourselves with those we admire, but from being at ease with oneself and one's surroundings (even one's shortcomings). . .and, above all, with one's God. Besides, as *Apples of Gold* says:

> *The person who worries over what other people think wouldn't worry half so much if he really knew how seldom he (or his home) is the subject of their thoughts.*

Freebies

While browsing through Costco the other day (or was it Sam's Club?), I spotted a friend nibbling her way through a maze of food sampling booths. Since, normally, this particular friend wouldn't be caught dead or alive enjoying a lowly hot dog, I sidled alongside her good ear.

"Having lunch?" I asked with a grin.

Holding a dollop of fat-free frozen entree loaded with sodium in one hand, she downed a minute flap of pizza before staring at me as if I were one Fruit Loop shy of a full bowl.

"Why not? It's free."

A week or so later, I had taken a break from shopping, grabbed a quick pretzel, and was slurping diet cola through a straw when another of my peers called out for a world of shoppers to hear, "How come you're eating here? Sodas are free today at Chompies!"

Knowing that a simple, "Because here is where I happen to be shopping," would make no sense to this honored citizen turned freebie-jeebie, I smiled and saved my breath.

That very weekend, my partner-for-life came home from a symposium bearing, not gifts, but a pile of vendor come-ons that included five key chains.

"Why, when we own but two vehicles and already have dealer key chains, Disney key chains, and key chains with pictures of the grandkids—to say nothing of all those key chains you brought home from that last meeting? What made you think we needed more?" I asked.

Without so much as a shrug or a sheepish look, he tossed the key chains among the litter on his side of the dresser. "They were free."

"It doesn't cost anything to bring home a sinus infection either, but it sure can fill up your head," I reminded this man whose drawers were already so crammed with giveaway items he barely had room to stuff his socks.

The mail came along about then, and with it—you've guessed it—promises for three more freebies. Flipping aside a packet of artistically challenged and free-for-a-donation greeting cards and an offer for a free estimate toward the cost of replacing a roof no older than our five-year-old house, I unearthed the third and only free offer that interested me.

The brochure was guaranteed to entice even the most discriminating of book lovers; some unknown-to-me book place was offering five free books along with free book club membership for as long as one ordered no less than two books a month. Never mind that I already belonged to two book clubs and owned books I had never read.

I snatched up a pen and was about to circle my five free choices when I saw that the owner of many key chains was now staring accusingly at me.

"They're—" I began. I stopped before I could utter that space-invading word that rhymes with "whee."

We were not finished with the "free" word, however. Not with a card in my freebie-lover's wallet bearing nine punches and the promise of a tenth meal on the house. We headed off to our complementary meal, though as things turned out, our taste buds were somewhat less than tickled by the free meal.

On the way home, I couldn't help but ponder: What good is a freebie if it's something we neither need nor truly want?

FOOD FOR THOUGHT

What boggles my mind is the fact that many of the folks who drive twenty miles for a free two-liter of pop have heard from childhood about a gift they've never bothered to accept. Which hardly makes sense in light of the fact that this Gift of all gifts has been around for a long time, bears a Name you can trust—and it's free!

Stuff 'n' Nonsense

It is not always true that one man's junk is another man's treasure. There are those who keep stuff for its value as a keepsake while others keep stuff for the sake of keeping stuff. After scrounging for two days, looking for an item that is still lost, I think I have identified my group. Among all that stuff I must once have thought valuable, I found only a few treasures and a whole lot of junk and useless cardboard, most of it musty.

If anyone knows how to stuff a house or garage with junk, it is those of us who are over sixty. We might as well face it: Most of us tend to view memorabilia as the one infallible umbilical cord linking past with future. What we forget is that God designed the umbilical cord not only to nourish but ultimately to be discarded.

Discarding, of course, is the hard part. What if I throw away something of value? An item my kids may want? A gift from some infrequent flyer who drops out of the sky and catches my neighbor carting the said treasure to her house from mine following a yard sale designed for doing away with doodads?

Placed strategically, a pile of magazines can simplify decor and eliminate the need for dusting doodads. Still, like those neighbors who annually share their zucchini, magazines just keep coming and coming. True, a few may one day make it onto somebody's list of collectibles. Precious few. None in my lifetime. I know, because my dad collected newspapers, and to date, not one has ever been seen on *Antiques Road Show.* Yet, who among us has dared to part with those molding stacks of *National Geographic* magazines and *Reader's Digest* condensed books? Stacks too big to keep and too good to throw away?

Houses once came equipped with attics and basements that held trunks and toys, widgets, and wedding dresses. You could stuff stuff there, and, if you got lucky, the mice or the descendants—or both—would take care of it. Alas! Houses are no longer being built with giant hidey-holes for sentimental stash; now we have bonus rooms. Since, sooner or later, bonus rooms get turned into air-conditioned offices and bedrooms, it's small wonder we keepers of family treasure have become a generation of messies.

Frankly, I get suspicious whenever I set foot in a house free of clutter. How many doors had to be shut in order to hide their fair share? What lurks behind the flounce of a sofa? Or fills the dead space behind books on a shelf?

Nothing as big as what's left of my husband's old hobbyhorse or Grandma's Flower Garden quilt, that's for sure. There's no space left in those rooms, in fact, big enough to hold what's accumulated from Norm's and my combined pasts. I wonder, have they, like the children of Ogden Nash, dug a hole in the backyard and inscribed an epithet?

Here lies my past,
Good-bye I have kissed it;
Thank you, kids,
I wouldn't have missed it.

Nash must not have believed, as some do, that a person's worth depends on how much stuff she has.

FOOD FOR THOUGHT

Come to think of it, since nothing but what matters to Christ will last, maybe we should treat stuff like we cull overripe fruit—preserve only what's best for whichever of our offspring might genuinely like a little flavor from the past.

Part 6

KIN CONNECTIONS

"I will pour out my Spirit on your offspring,
and my blessing on your descendants.
They will spring up like grass in a meadow,
like poplar trees by flowing streams.
One will say, 'I belong to the Lord'. . .
still another will write on his hand, 'The LORD's.' "
ISAIAH 44:3–5

Heir Raising

Grandparenting at its delightful best means that we no longer need to play the heavy. If a dead snake graces a reception via the pocket of a grandson or a granddaughter shows up wearing an outfit more suited to barn mucking, I can smile or sigh in peace. Still, while it is up to their parents to act, react, or ignore, I take grandparenting seriously.

While blessed by good parents whose energy and foresight provided me with siblings one short of a dozen, I was never fortunate enough to meet my own grandparents. Due to a variety of circumstances, our children never got to see a whole lot of their grandparents either. Now that it's my turn, though, I've placed grandparenting near the top of my priority list.

For sure, grandparenting got my full attention the day a

grandson showed up at a family gathering sprouting a gold ring from a hole drilled into one tortured ear. I really paid attention when his cousin interpreted the piercing as a family tradition.

I couldn't help but think of the rings my farmer father sometimes attached to the snouts of overzealous pigs. "You can't make a silk purse out of a—"

The culprit grinned. "Yeah, Grandma. If God meant for people to smoke, He'd have made them with chimneys and, uh, with holes in their ears. Hey, the earring was free—ten bucks for piercing."

He thought he knew a bargain when he saw one, and I, for sure, knew when to shut up.

The truth concerning grandkids is this: While they may be smarter and better looking than any other kids, they are still going to drag in mangy puppies and a few will undoubtedly flub exams. Most will watch too much television, blast out their only set of eardrums, and take turns looking like something the cat drug in. Some will sleep through job opportunities, spend allowances in advance, and barf up their broccoli. A few will even dare to sass you.

So, what's a grandparent to do now that she has lived long enough to get a good handle on the sometimes devastating permanence of cause and effect?

To borrow a term from a grandkid or three—loosen up. I did, and what do you know? One silly earring disappeared near the start of a new romance and the other upon onset of physical pain.

Being a grandparent is not about parenting or censorship. It is a God-given role that offers an opportunity to give oneself to the people who mean the most to us.

To our grandchildren, we are the owners of heirlooms and the source of their history; we provide added applause at school programs and a postcard from Portland. We are soft pillows, home-baked cookies, and the hoarse voice after ball games. We listen to them brag, treat them as individuals, and serve "real" mashed potatoes. Possibly, we can help them see their parents as human beings. We are the playmates who offer security, help with chores, give second opinions (unbiased), and can read nine books aloud at a sitting.

Our homes welcome our grandchildren and model Christian values. We pray daily for them and have hearts and ears attuned to hear their spiritual needs. What few rules we have are sensible, fair, and enforced. As for poor grades, dead snakes, and other nonsense—well, they're really not our problems. (Thank the Lord!)

FOOD FOR THOUGHT

The Bible says, "Train a child in the way he should go, and when he is old he will not turn from it" (Proverbs 22:6). We've already done that. Now it's our kids' turn.

Wrapping It Up

'Twas the season to be both generous and jolly. Since it was Tuesday, the day when most stores offer a senior discount, aisles were jammed with customers, all of us shamelessly admitting our age in order to claim the discount.

Arms loaded, I was standing in line listening to a piped rendition of "Joy to the Mall, the Card Has Come" (or some such garbled version of a Christmas carol), when a friend joined me.

As I explained that several new babies in the span of one year had doubled the number of our grandchildren, she stared at me, then blurted, "Surely you don't buy for all of them!"

"Well," I said, repressing laughter, "it would be tough deciding which one to leave out."

Still, my friend had a point. Stretching a fixed income to buy gifts for grandkids who appear to already have everything can be a challenge. It can also make you a little hard-nosed.

While I love giving good gifts to our grandchildren, I cannot keep straight what name or logo should appear on which school bag or seat of whose jeans. I don't even try. Chances are, I couldn't afford sixteen of them anyhow.

Furthermore, I am not responsible for making sure their Christmas wish lists come true. I did that already with my own kids. Wish-granting is now their parents' job. Besides, with granddaughters who copy whole pages (complete with order numbers) from a toy catalog and a grandson whose list reads like a Gart Bros. inventory, who can afford to look at lists? (In fairness, he did write, "Just kidding, Grandma," beside *motorcycle*.)

Even if we could afford the highest-priced item on each of their lists (which we usually cannot), why not instead give small gifts that children can experience, use up, or simply enjoy:

- A gift certificate for a favorite fast-food or pizza restaurant. (Check out those favorites in advance!)
- Tickets for wholesome entertainment, such as the

zoo or a Christian concert.

- Lunch out for just the two or three of you.
- Subscription to a Christian magazine.
- Devotional or other books chosen with each
  child's interests in mind.

While I once caught my neighbor, a grandmother of forty-two grandchildren, purchasing thirteen identical dolls, buying in quantity is seldom the way to shop for gifts. Better to consider each child individually, even if we must get to know them through phone calls or E-mail.

Consider, too, those gifts that only a grandparent can give. Young people will thrill over a gift of old coins, jewelry, or other keepsakes that have been handed down through the family. Make or buy a special box for each gift and include a handwritten account of how each came to be a family treasure.

Buy a blank book with a pretty cloth cover and write down your family stories. If possible, include snapshots of the parent who grew up in your home. Or put together a small photo album of family pictures selected just for your grandchild. Have you hung on to those old slides? For a more costly but long-lasting family gift, select the best and have them put on videotape, complete with a narrative.

These items may not be on your grandchildren's lists —but they are nevertheless precious gifts that only a grandparent can give.

FOOD FOR THOUGHT

Even if we don't have a dime to spend on our grandchildren, the gift of a fine heritage will out-last any fast-fad trinket we can buy. So will sharing the greatest Gift of all.

And unlike the heap of stuff we accumulate as we tramp all over town and trek the malls, eternal gifts don't have to be wrapped.

Missed Manners

The person who suggested that cold cash or a store-wrapped gift keeps one in touch with the latest bride or one's own descendants must never read "Dear Abby." According to folks who thrive on columnizing their favorite gripes, there's hardly a grandkid or newlywed alive who takes the time to say thank you. To write or phone those two magic words is unheard of.

The advice varies with the unthanked occasion and goes something like this:

- Refuse to put up with it.
- Shop no more.
- Grab the checkbook; pinch those ingrates off at the signature.

- Phone the parents and ask if their recently wed offspring living five states away received monogrammed napkins from you via the Big Dollar Store, or did they not.

Whoa! Doesn't the bottom line of good manners have to do with one's ability to put up with the bad manners of others? While it is quite possible to give without loving (for the sake of appearance and duty), how can we love without giving? Those columnists have a lot to learn. Our Lord said not to worry; if there was getting even to be done, He'd take care of it (Romans 12:19).

Failing to express thanks is not merely a fault of the current generation of young people. No, this is a fault that's been around a good long while. A prime example is the tale of ten fellows who stopped Jesus in the middle of a journey with their hollering. After Jesus healed their ten ailing hides, only one had the grace to return and thank Him (Luke 17:11–19).

Since a tenth of a gain belongs to the Lord, could the nine have figured one thank-you sufficient? Were they ungrateful? Probably not. More likely they were simply careless and forgetful and excited over what had happened to them. At any rate, while Jesus acknowledged the one and asked about the others, the record doesn't indicate that He wrote off the other nine.

The truth is that with Jesus the giving never stops. He gives and gives again, and who among us has thanked Him enough?

Still, no one is especially blessed by a thankless child. So what's a person to do?

This pinches, but they say (or someone *ought* to say!) if you want to reform a man (or a negligent bride or a thankless grandkid), you've got to begin with the grandmother. No problem. This grandma gave birth to five children, all of whom can embellish identical stories of having been plunked down to write thank-yous while every other kid on the planet was outdoors playing. Furthermore, among my treasures are enough smudged epistles to prove that they, too, were "mean moms" and made their children do the same.

With no additional help from me, my kids grew up and learned to say thank you on their own. Their kids probably will, too. Likewise, those errant brides and some others I care enough about to give gifts to will, too.

And if they don't? Hey, this fading butterfly must confess to having had caterpillar days of her own. Some of us just take longer than others to grow our wings.

FOOD FOR THOUGHT

Since the carelessness of youth is an ailment from which most of us eventually recover, a new twist on an old Scripture seems apropos: "Do not let your left hand know what your right hand is doing" (Matthew 6:3). Stop waiting to be paid by thank-yous, and you need never again fret over a phone that fails to ring or a mailbox that's empty of thank-you notes. Give for the simple joy of giving! As someone has said, "There's not a whole lot of grace in giving that which sticks to the fingers."

Play-off

Norm and I were not surprised when the most feminine of our family signed up for her school's annual powder puff football game. She was, after all, athletic.

On the day of the game, the crowd cheered as two teams of young ladies clad in uniforms designed for husky young men jogged onto the field. The girls doffed borrowed helmets and offered a snappy salute while a classmate sang "The Star-Spangled Banner." Then they tucked up their hair, trotted across close-clipped grass, and positioned themselves to play.

Encouraged by the donors of the uniforms, who, hairy legs and all, now masqueraded as cheerleaders, the ladies celebrated the first quarter with several mix-ups, a few time-outs, and a whole lot of whistle-blowing—but no score.

Throughout quarter number two, the ladies minimized mix-ups, increased whistle-blowings and time-outs, drew "for crying out louds" from the cheerleaders, and still did zilch for the score.

At halftime, the regular boys' squad pranced onto the field wearing sweatshirts and assorted pleated skirts belonging to their friends and moms and grandmothers. They formed a drill team and entertained the crowd with maximized mix-ups and more than a little silliness.

By the middle of third quarter, the cheerleaders had forgotten their role and were crowding the edge of the field, coaxing the girls to please do something. Anything? The drill team covered their eyes in unison and moaned. Still no score.

"Get back in there and fight!" bawled the coach as the girls struggled wearily onto the field for the final quarter. The game proceeded with little change.

Suddenly, our little fullback had the ball. Spying an opening, she darted between players with the speed of a Wyoming jackrabbit. The crowd went wild as in ragged V-formation, her teammates ran hollering after her.

They never caught up with her.

She made the only touchdown in the game—for the other team. She had the ball and she had her chance—and she ran the wrong way. The crowd got their money's worth; everyone had a good laugh at our small hero's expense; and she giggled for days at herself. After all, it was only a game.

But in the game we call life, it is no laughing matter to look helplessly on from the stands while grown-ups and young people we love aim carelessly toward the wrong goal. Or to hover powerless beneath warm stadium blankets of Truth while friends, siblings, and offspring run aimlessly around.

Such goings-on make us want to toot our whistles and fire the coach, to shake the Book in their faces and holler, or at least insist on a heart-to-heart time-out.

But listen, folks, we're neither helpless nor powerless. God has given us a powerful weapon we sometimes forget—prayer. And prayer can accomplish a whole lot more than anything else we might try.

FOOD FOR THOUGHT

According to Emily Dickinson,

Prayer is the little implement
Through which men reach
Where presence is denied them.

I think she means prayer is more likely to insti-
gate a turnaround than either time-outs or hollering. Still, if I'd been Emily, I'd have spent some
time with a thesaurus before ascribing "little" to
the whopping instrument we call prayer.

Reunion Notice

Last summer, after I'd sent invitations to each of my parents' descendants, several dozen of them journeyed to an Idaho church camp for a family reunion.

Not all of the remaining "originals" (my six sisters, my brother, and I) could make it. With one unable to venture beyond the comforts of a nursing home, their absence was understandable. Still, when another opted not to travel, the rest were disappointed. Once you realize you are the older generation, even the thought of a sibling's empty place can be scary.

The reunion site was closer to home for us than usual, so when the time came for family pictures, Norm and I scored a perfect seven: Every one of our children was there and accounted for. But before a battery of assorted cameras could trigger a passel of grandkids into making faces, a spouse had to leave and we were shy one of our sons-in-law. That, too, was disappointing. Still, we felt blessed—until we remembered our missing grandkid.

A wedding in need of a bridesmaid and assorted work schedules meant that the grandkids came late, left early, or stayed throughout, depending. Having a quiver nearly full should have been enough to launch Grandma into orbit. Not so! Not while one grandchild searched for a lost plane ticket more than sixteen hundred miles away.

Eventually, while laughing our heads off down at the lake, it occurred to me that ours was not the only grandkid absent. My sibling's grandchild had just missed seeing his older brother dump his family from canoe to water in less time than it took for an aunt to aim her camcorder; and he was too far away to hear a dripping toddler holler, "Do it again, Daddy!"

Saturday night someone arranged chairs and told us "originals" we should relay a few stories from the past to all who would listen. As we took turns telling how our mom, age nineteen and eight months' pregnant, had walked several steep and winding miles behind a wagon up White Bird Hill, a grandkid meandered outdoors.

No big deal, I suppose. My kids and grandkids have

heard my stories before and will likely hear them again. Still, as an eighty-five-year-young sibling began sharing memories that were new to me, I wondered, Was the kid searching for katydids among the wildflowers likely to get a second chance to hear her stories? After much prayer and twisting of amateur arms, we trekked over to the chapel on Sunday and cooperated in a first-ever family church service. With five denominations to please, planning took some doing. God honored our efforts in ways we could not have imagined.

While this happy camper tucked soggy tissues into jeans never before seen in church, some who normally don't took Communion, sang along with instruments, and listened to personal testimonies, perhaps for the first time. During those holy moments, I yearned for each of my grandkids and all who were even remotely related.

Family has to be one of God's best gifts. But the bigger a family grows, the harder it is for everyone to be in one place at the same time. Thankfully, geography and time schedules do not limit the Spirit's working. Even when loving arms and familiar smiles are far away, God's love can still unite us.

FOOD FOR THOUGHT

Who among those we love will miss out on the grandest reunion of all, the one that will last for all eternity? Have we offered directions or helped anyone to locate their "missing ticket"?

Has everyone been invited?

Eye Spy

Woe unto those of us who managed to survive several wars when our children begin to suspect we've crested the hill and have started to slide. They don't need sufficient grounds for their suspicion. If a grown child catches you in some senseless act that may or may not have to do with your age, you might as well mark it down on the calendar where you keep all that other stuff you know you've got to remember. Mark my words, and mark them in black, because your children are not going to forget. From that day forward, they will watch for signs.

So, what if you never married? Bore no children? All I can say is, watch your step around nieces and nephews or even younger siblings and acquaintances. The minute they exchange that first knowing look, life will be no different for you than for parents of offspring. Surveillance of the aging begins with the small stuff.

A dollop of mustard slithers off your hamburger during a family barbecue and lands on the front of your white T-shirt. It can happen to anyone (in fact, often does). You, however, are over sixty. So the grown kids look at each other. If any were to comment, they would probably say something like: "Have you noticed? Grandma's started dribbling her food down her front." Or, "We'd better keep an eye on Dad; make sure he wears a clean shirt in public."

Further, the generation some of us took twenty years or more to rear has no savvy when it comes to our likes and dislikes. The assumption seems to be that we who grew up during the golden days of radio are too far gone to understand what goes on during the latest sitcoms in the name of humor. We understand it all right. So well it sickens us. As for remembering the names of today's movie stars, I plead guilty of total lack of recall. It's more in keeping with my lifestyle to try to recall which prophet it was, Elijah or Elisha, who watched those bears come out of the woods and tear into the kids for making fun of his bald head.

True, the memory does eventually balk when it strives for instant recall. But face it: We have a lot of things to remember.

It you really want to scare your kids into leafing through the yellow pages beneath the heading marked nursing homes, try mixing the names of siblings or cousins. Forget, momentarily, the name of your latest grandbaby and watch how quickly those to whom you gave birth glance knowingly at each other. Never mind that you've just cooked dinner for twenty-four while keeping in mind that one grandkid is allergic to chocolate, another can't stand broccoli, your second child is dieting, and somebody's fiancé doesn't like. . . What's more, you've taken time to greet each arrival, ooh and ah over the newest baby, look at all the latest snapshots, and still the food is all on the table on time. The hot is still hot and the cold is cold. You even have presence of mind enough to say a decent blessing if called upon to do so.

So from time to time, I remind myself of these facts with just a bit of righteous indignation. And meanwhile, my daughters eyeball each other every time I happen to button my blouse crooked.

FOOD FOR THOUGHT

Thinking about all those sidelong glances and the

amount of attention paid to dribbles and such, I suppose it's my own fault. I did what the Bible said: I brought up my children in the way they should go. So it can hardly be their fault they grew up caring about their mother.

Part 7

NOTIONS AND NOSTALGIA

Whatever is has already been,
and what will be has been before;
and God will call the past to account.
ECCLESIASTES 3:15

Streets and Alleys

Meetings are not on the list of things I do best. Let a discussion fall below the cutting edge, and my mind wanders off down a path of related ideas.

At one such meeting, after we had dead-ended on whether or not a person might be offended if asked to sign a church guest register, I mentally found myself back beside a country lane, waiting for the ride that would take me to church. . . .

According to statistics, kids who attend church without their parents seldom do well spiritually. That being true, those who picked me up for Sunday school should not have been wasting their time. Furthermore, once there, I managed to commit every kid-style, anti-worship atrocity I could think of in record time. I sneered at the soloist and giggled aloud during prayer; I dropped marbles. I ran in the sanctuary, got called down, sat with, and more. If that small church had owned a guest book, I could have signed it "Huckleberry Herdman" with honesty and aplomb. (In Barbara Robinson's delightful book, *The Best Christmas Pageant Ever,* the Herdmans were absolutely the worst kids in the history of Sunday school.)

Evidently, those good folks who brought me to church were not up on statistics. People hugged me and said, "See you next week," as if I'd keep coming there forever.

Norm and I got married, moved to a new community, and neglected to choose a church. But before long, Bob and Rose came through the hedge surrounding our apartment house and knocked on our door. Rose said, "Why not come have a peanut butter and tomato sandwich with us?"

Although we both took our peanut butter straight, we slid the tomatoes to one side and got to know each other. Bob said they'd see us in church in the morning.

Maybe that church foyer sported a guest book; I don't know. All I remember is folks asking our names and knowing we mattered to them. Art and Esther invited us for watermelon on Thursday.

Since none of us owned a television, no one had any reason to hurry home following the evening service. So

Don and Martha said for us and Art and Esther and Bob and Rose to come on over; we'd make popcorn.

Our new friends spoke of Jesus with ease, as if each considered Him a personal friend. Talk about wanting what belonged to your neighbor! After some of the older folks had us over for dinner and demonstrated how sweet life with Christ could be at forty and at sixty, we were hooked.

Then someone found Leland and Patty living near a street corner north of the church. I made iced tea and chocolate chip cookies; we told our friends to come over, and we got a good start on loving those two into the church.

Later on, after we all had two or three kids and needed some Sunday school equipment, we called all the parents who didn't come with their kids and asked if they'd help us build tables. We had a potluck and hammered and painted tables, and some of those parents came back every Sunday.

With a sigh, I stopped wool gathering and discovered the committee had gotten off guest books and onto Velcro-backed daisies for the collar or lapel. With effort, I refrained from hollering like a Herdman about how I used to chew the corner off a collar faster than my mother could sew one and would've choked on a posy for sure. Besides, since our church guests consisted almost entirely of our own out-of-town relatives, why all the flap?

Thinking back, although folks asked my name first thing and remembered it, I still can't place any guest books among the pages of my early spiritual history. I recall with gratitude, however, those who understood Matthew 22:9 and Luke 14:23. These were people who knew the true meaning of the phrase "streets and alleys."

FOOD FOR THOUGHT

Times have changed. "Doing church" incognito is in, and all our fences and freeways make it hard to see the hedges. With three videos to return by Monday morning, hardly anyone has time to smear peanut butter for a Herdman. Even popcorn comes in single-serving bags these days.

Maybe it's time to change all that. Sharing the gospel really isn't all that complicated. It just means shifting our focus to the things that really matter. Things like learning people's names and sharing potluck.

February Focus

The tale told to me by my first-grade teacher of heart-shaped messages slid between Roman prison bars may be only a story. Further, Valentine's Day may even have a pagan origin.

Christian love, however, is more than legendary. Even those who know nothing of its Source, can easily recognize the love that ventures forth as caregiver, consoler, cook, and carpenter—love that baby-sits, paints, binds wounds, and more. A few years ago, this same love came to me from an unlikely source following a February storm.

I knew I was in trouble the minute the snow tires hit the easternmost route around Salt Lake City. I had just left a prayer meeting, and since Norm was off troubleshooting for his company in Boise, I found myself all alone in a blinding sea of rapidly falling snow. Gripping the steering wheel, I prayed my way over the trackless mountainside freeway and backed up five times before I could convince my car that yes, we had made it to the right turnoff. The crazy vehicle didn't even recognize our driveway. Nor did it seem to understand that broadside is an impossible angle for a Mustang to enter a garage.

The next morning I donned boots and mittens and began moving snowdrifts as high as the hood ornament. Pausing to rest, I could hear the rhythmic scraping of several shovels.

A door slammed across the street. Two men with snow shovels surveyed their clogged walkway. New to our neighborhood, they spoke no English. *More of those foreign Mormon converts,* I surmised. I shoveled on.

Unable to keep up the pace, my shovel leaning turned into a senior sag. Then I noticed that the grandma in my driveway—me—had become the subject of gesturing across the street. Under the guise of wiping sweat, I glanced past a soggy mitten and figured the two must be cracking little old lady jokes over my spasmodic efforts to unearth a driveway. I turned my back and began shoveling for all I was worth—which, by now, wasn't much.

Suddenly, the men were working beside me. Without so

much as an unintelligible word, within minutes, my driveway was clean. The youngest of the two grabbed a broom and began sweeping snow from my car, then stopped.

Pointing to the Bible I had forgotten and left on the front seat, grinning happily, he drew an unmistakable cross in the frosty air. He touched his ski jacket, then pointed in turn toward my heart. I nodded, he nodded, and the other fellow nodded, and we all stood there smiling our faces off, slaphappy with the joy of recognition. I had kept my distance from my new neighbors, but they had reached out anyway, witnesses to Christ's love.

Later, after Norm came home, I was inspired by our new neighbors' example. I baked and frosted a birthday cake, and we drove over to see some lonely old folks we know. Norm took care of some simple repairs while I washed up a few dishes. We admired their treasures and listened for awhile to their stories. Then we opened up some ice cream, lit a few candles, and helped celebrate an eighty-ninth birthday. Maybe we brought a little happiness; we certainly received enough to fill our hearts to the brim.

Though my winter helpers spoke a different language, they had successfully taught me an important message about love.

FOOD FOR THOUGHT

My new neighbors knew I shared their Savior
when they saw my Bible inside my car. But even
the smallest act of love beats a cold Bible lying
prone on a car seat. After all—"They will know
we are Christians by our love."

Best Christmas Ever

My best Christmas ever happened the year I married the light of my life, invited the Light of the World into my heart, and bought our first in a long and fizzling string of tree lights. Before that, my best Christmas had to be the year my friends all got Shirley Temple dolls and my mother gave me a dollar with which to buy gifts.

To folks who deal in credit cards faster than I could ever shuffle a deck of Old Maid, I must explain. We were not poor. Like countless families surviving the Great Depression, we simply had no money.

So when Mom handed me a worn dollar bill in the middle of Chattie Kester's Variety and said, "Seven is old enough to think about presents for someone other than yourself," you could have blown me over with a tin whistle.

Long after she had gone across the street to Vic's Grocery, I walked those creaky board aisles, deciding how best to spend such wealth.

The trouble was, while Mom had said I needn't worry about gifts for my away siblings, our at-home family still numbered nine. Buying the twenty-five-cent box of embroidered handkerchiefs for Mom and a green rubber car for my baby brother, left but fifty cents for the remaining six.

I had already raided Mom's scrap bag to make pen wipes for Dad. Using a blunt stub pencil or a pen dipped in royal blue ink that sometimes bled, Dad always wrote in calligraphy. No matter how many lint-free wipes we made for him, Dad could always use more.

By the time Mom returned, the handkerchiefs and rubber car lay in a bag alongside fake red nail polish and a celluloid doll for the sisters just older and younger than myself. The bag also held some kite string.

At home, divided by only a supper table from the four for whom I had no gifts, I decided to wrap IOUs and, when March came, share my kite string. Later, though, watching my nimble-fingered mother pick meats from a pan of cracked hickory nuts, I came up with a better idea.

Hickory nuts grew on our timber-covered farm—and

they were free. While we all liked nuts, however, my brothers were lazy about cracking their own, and my older sisters hated hunching over the cracking block in a frigid winter woodshed.

Three cold afternoons and a couple of thumb-numbing triple-whammies later, I sat beside Mom and pretended to help pick nutmeats for the aunts. Since my fingers were not as deft as hers, by Christmas Eve day, I had only a half-cup of nuts to show for my efforts.

Dumping the nutmeats into an empty baking soda box, I divided what remained (shells and all) into three lumpy packages. As I tucked those homely gifts beneath the tree alongside the pen wipes and my store-bought packages, my heart swelled. I think I knew at that moment that "the best gifts are tied with heartstrings."

That night, for the first time, I sat with legs dangling off an unfamiliar pew and watched a Sunday school class pantomime the story of Jesus' birth. As the pastor prayed and thanked God for giving to all the gift of His only Son, my offerings beneath a lopsided cedar tree suddenly seemed puny. Especially those nuts still stuck in their cracked little shells.

The next day, my brothers exchanged glances, and said, "Uh. . .thanks." The sister holding the baking soda box murmured, "Yum," and the other said, "Wow, already cracked, no less." I smiled, filled with the bliss of having spent my dollar wisely. I had given my seven-year-old best.

FOOD FOR THOUGHT

Today, with multiple dollars to spend, I still find
that "God's gifts put our best dreams to shame"
(to paraphrase Elizabeth Barrett Browning).

Children's Hour

Once upon a time, I knew next to nothing about remembering the Sabbath day and even less about keeping it. "Holy" had to do with the heels and toes of my constantly moving socks. Still, I liked Sunday, the one day of the week when Mom closed the lid on her sewing machine and let the hoe dangle from its peg on the backside of our old-fashioned washhouse. Sundays were when Dad saddled Old Babe, and we could ride just for the fun of it. On Sundays no canning jars had to be lugged from the cellar, and Mom had no buckets of beans for us to snap.

Cows still had to be milked, of course, and the sheep tended, along with other chores. Then, while Dad checked floodgates and rode fences, Mom stirred up a sunshine cake or maybe some blackberry cobbler, fried three or four chickens, and pulled, peeled, buttered, sliced, and mashed succulent mounds of potatoes and other vegetables.

Following the kind of dinner many during those Great Depression days knew nothing about, we did dishes and jumped rope or played Simon Says while our parents took naps that sometimes lasted as excruciatingly late as 4 P.M.

After that, anything could happen. Sunday evening chores got reduced to a minimum, and they were done in a hurry. In summertime, while we all stood listening for the crack that invariably ran ahead of her knife, Mom might cut the striped watermelon she'd had cooling in the shade. Or Dad could disappear inside a sawdust-filled shed straddling our tiny creek and come out carrying a gunny-sack filled with pond ice; we all knew that meant we'd soon be enjoying Mom's home-cranked ice cream.

Winters, we played Authors or Uncle Wiggly, made popcorn and molasses taffy, and supped on apple slices and bowls of crusty homemade bread soaked in creamy milk. Before bed, Dad read aloud from a Zane Grey novel.

Small wonder a single verse penned by Longfellow made me think of him as a friend who knew our family well:

Between the dark and the daylight,
When the light is beginning to lower,

Comes a pause in the day's occupations
That is known as the Children's Hour.

Back then, I had my own distorted picture of God, an old man who worked for six days and rested for one. Like my great-uncle Isaac, God had a beard that fanned in the breeze while He lolled on a cloud through that whole seventh day. God ate, goofed around, and on Monday went back to work.

When I finally got around to meeting God, He far exceeded my image of Him. Sunday, however, turned out to be as good as ever, if a bit busier than I experienced as a child. While the workweek may come to a halt, like the luminous hands on Mom's trusty alarm clock, chore time still rolls around, but today's Sunday chores are loving, caring, serving kinds of chores. Teaching, tending, ushering, counting, and more. If all are to feast, then many must prepare and serve.

It turns out, though, that naps have their rightful place.

As for the warm, fuzzy feeling I experienced while swinging from the back of Dad's rocker, listening to tales of scalpings and buffalo stampedes, I can't help but think he missed the greatest literature ever when he failed to read to us from the Bible.

Nevertheless, those were good times. Today Sunday evening is still a deliciously simple bowl of bread with milk —a buttery-popcorn kind of a time filled with the possibility of growing closer to God and my church family.

I guess I'm still a kid at heart. I still like the Children's Hour.

FOOD FOR THOUGHT

Sunday, according to Joseph Addison, clears away the "rust" of the week. If you add worship and the Word, then the day truly offers a fresh beginning to Monday.

Smitten Image

Some say that after a couple has been married for awhile the two start to look like each other. I don't think so. More than fifty years have scampered by since I stood with my best friend before a silver-haired preacher, and the two of us murmured vows that would bind us together through thick paychecks and thin. To date, no fly has ever left skid marks across my scalp, and, unlike me, the man who vacuums on my behalf remains unwrinkled. Still, although he wears a full mop of hair only on his chin and my hair covers the rest of my head, we do manage to fill our days with behave-alike stuff that has nothing to do with our looks.

Take the sentence. Any sentence. Long, short, simple, or compound. If one of us starts it, the other can finish it right down to action verbs and punctuation. What's more, while outmaneuvering one's partner is a bit tricky, we can do the same with thoughts. The process goes something like this:

Each year, come early October, I begin mentally flailing myself. I don't say a word, but after we've had a couple of extra frosty mornings, I finish my last swallow of breakfast coffee, open my mouth, and the man of my dreams says, "Yeah, I know, it's time to wash the outside windows."

Or it works the other way around; I catch a glimpse of what he is thinking and say, "Just go buy it." He says, "Are you sure?" and meanwhile neither of us has said a word to identify the doohickey I have just given him the go-ahead to purchase.

What we are really both good at, however, is out-shuffling. Out-shuffling, I'm convinced, is a skill best perfected by those who dwell in close proximity, preferably over long periods of time. To develop finesse, one must first study the out-shuffling maneuvers of the other out-shuffler.

He, for instance, is single-minded when it comes to refrigerator shelves. He looks at the contents to the forefront of the one refrigerator shelf he can easily see and fails to find the orange marmalade. He sighs, and I, while I know I am being out-shuffled, stoop, bend, and retrieve the marmalade jar from the turntable where it sits every day.

I, on the other hand, have trouble balancing the

checkbook; I count on Norm to correct my errors. I also know that if I leave clean dishes in a gaping dishwasher, my most significant someone will put them away. It works every time.

He has known from day one of our union how many days of procrastination are needed to avoid ever having to write letters to his mom or to anyone else. In a good marriage, of course, you keep things in balance. While he is not writing letters, I am busy not getting the hang of jerk-starting the power lawn mower. I may forever be equally helpless when faced with a gas pump. He gets me back, however; were it not for toast, coffee, and boxed macaroni and cheese, the man who cheerfully eats my cooking could easily starve if left on his own too long.

Much of our out-shuffling has to do with our differing roles. No matter how many years we rack up, my favorite roommate and I are never going to look alike for one obvious reason: He's a guy and I am (to use the term loosely) a girl. It's how God made us. We like it that way.

FOOD FOR THOUGHT

For more than fifty years, my husband and I have

been united in our allegiance to the Lord we both love. Still, I don't think baking a cake fit for a new family on the block has ever been a part of his plans. And I, for sure, am not about to jockey all over town in a wheezing old Sunday school bus. But if loving God with your whole heart and mind, body and soul, and your neighbor as yourself gives folks even a little glimpse of Jesus, then maybe we do look alike.

Celebrations

"Where have the years gone?" we asked each other the day we began celebrating our first fifty years of having daily brushed our teeth over the same sink.

While I don't know where either the good or the bad times go once they've been used up, I do know the years allotted to us have been marked by rough roads and smooth. Furthermore, if years were to be handed tickets for speeding, someone would be paying a big fine.

Unlike those fast-flying years, our once-in-a-lifetime celebration began early and moseyed along for three or four months. Now, more than two years later, only the indestructible memories remain.

The kids got together and forged plans for a wingding that will stick in our minds (assuming we can hang onto them) for the rest of our days. "Reception or retreat?" they asked us a year or so in advance.

Aware of what quick work sixteen grandkids were likely to make of anything their mothers could pile onto one reception table, and knowing some might never drive that far to stay dressed up for that long, we said, "Retreat."

What happened after must surely have taken both time and effort on the part of our offspring. It will be fully appreciated only by those who, at one time or another, have jock-eyed around summer jobs and school schedules in order to get thirty or more people together long enough to properly fete the two responsible for their existence.

They all came, including May and June's newlyweds and at least one grandson who might rather have been skateboarding. For two whole days we played and prayed, slept and ate, and felt blessed to spend time hobnobbing with the sum total of our descendants together beneath one sheet metal roof.

The kids and their kids all went home, and at last the day came when we really had been married for fifty years. We gussied up in our best outfits, pinned flowers on each other, and enjoyed dinner alongside folks dressed in ragged shorts and T-shirts on the terrace of a spendy restaurant. At home, we read through the stack of anniversary cards a daughter had collected and tied with gold ribbon.

A few days later, we packed up our duds and took off on a honeymoon kind of a trip, one day of which we might barely have afforded when our journey as partners began. We scarfed hot dogs from street vendors, sampled shoofly pie in Pennsylvania, ordered lunch from a French menu (and got all the right stuff), buttered bagels in motel rooms, and, in the name of dinner, stared into the beady eyes of freshly steamed lobsters.

We walked on the floor of the Atlantic, climbed a small mountain, and strolled through russet leaves carpeting Robert Frost's woods. A thirty-dollar pass got us into "Anne of Green Gables" country via the longest bridge in the world, and Longfellow's "Evangeline" came alive near the shores of the Acadian exile. We saw puffins and paintings, covered bridges and a castle, tinsmiths and tunnels, and the inside of a whole lot of stores (definitely not Norm's favorite part of the trip).

We were somewhere on a boat, viewing a scattering of mansions built by the bygone rich and famous when it occurred to me that I, that very day, had another anniversary to celebrate, and that I, too—though I will never be rich or famous—have a mansion in my future, a mansion of far greater dimensions than all of those forty-or-so-room monstrosities combined.

We didn't wear flowers or open any cards. The kids weren't there, and for atmosphere we settled for outdoor stools near a dockside burger joint. Dinner consisted of coleslaw on a paper plate alongside a cheeseburger. But I knew that the anniversary of the day I gave my life to Jesus was one well worth celebrating.

FOOD FOR THOUGHT

We may have privately and quietly celebrated the dedication of our lives to God—but I have a feeling that fifty years of sitting at the feet of the Master had a whole lot to do with Norm's and my marriage lasting long enough to merit the more public celebration our children gave us.

Pot Licked

Potlucks, covered-dish suppers, shared affairs—whatever you call them, wherever your locale, they have rarely, to me, meant keen cuisine.

This could have to do with the way I was raised. My father (being of the old school) believed children should be seldom seen and heard even less. He also thought kids should be last in line.

The picture I have in my mind of the annual Sunday school picnic—food spread in mouthwatering abundance over tables lugged beneath giant shade trees in the center of a park—is not the same as it must be for the forty or so other kids who got to be first in line. While those lucky ducks jabbed each other with assorted forks and the Sunday school superintendent prayed, I bowed my head and counted through my fingers the long queue of adults separating me and my siblings from what looked to my young eyes like a mountain of food.

By the time my turn came to choose, my freckles had turned pale with hunger and there was not one shred of potato salad left. Two chocolate-covered marshmallow cookies graced the plate of a boy from my school, but I knew in advance there were none left for me. Even my half glass of lemonade, laced with seventeen seeds, came from the bottom of the jar.

Hardly anything changed during the early years of marriage and family. While Dad no longer directed my manners before meals, I now had the baby to feed and plates to fill for however many other kids we had at the moment. By the time I got to the food, there was spaghetti in the coleslaw, beet pickle juice dribbled over the one lone chicken back, and potato chips floated in the fruit punch.

The year we lived in the country, several neighbors decided to get together for a cooperative dinner at the schoolhouse. Having promised myself that this time things would be different, I called a baby-sitter, cooked a couple of special dishes, and packed table service for two.

How quickly one forgets!

I don't know how it works now, but at a Midwestern

dinner back then, the men went first, kids second, and older ladies third. We who had done the cooking scraped pot bottoms and made do with whatever failed the palate test for those who had gone before.

Once at a church potluck, a well-meaning person passed before me bearing a plate heaped with goodies, the flavor of which I could only imagine, and commented, "Haven't we got the best cooks in the whole world?"

I murmured a church-appropriate, gracious reply, asked the Lord to forgive my lying tongue, and begged Him to keep me from hollering a most un-churchy "How would I know?" in the direction of her ample back.

Years later, when for some forgotten reason it became my lot to be first in line, I could scarcely handle the honor. All those beautiful bowls and platters of food! Why, there were rolls in the basket and steam rising from the meat loaf. Parsley stood like a Green Beret sentinel, guarding a creamy dish of macaroni salad, and nine untouched pies awaited my choice.

Moments later, I carried my filled plate to a table and sat down. At last, my turn had come. All good things really do come to those who wait long enough.

FOOD FOR THOUGHT

When I think of potluck dinners, I can't help but think of something Jesus once said.

He said that folks would show up from every direction on earth and that the whole kit and kaboodle will have a place set just for them at His feast. He also warned that the last will be first and the first might as well know right up front that they're going to be last.

Since being first at a single potluck should scarcely be counted, I can hardly wait!

At Ease

Inertia, according to Webster, is "a tendency to remain in a fixed condition without change; a disinclination to move or to act." Sounds to me like a rite of passage into the land that lies beyond age sixty.

The first clue that aging has to do with more than moldy cheese bags in a cave, in fact, may simply be a greater desire to nap. True, folks of all ages take naps—just not while other people are watching. Those graceless, unplanned moments have been reserved, I suspect, for those of us who are over sixty.

Somebody asked me the other day if I thought we ought to slow down because we're getting older or hurry up because we're not getting any younger. I didn't know we had a choice.

As suggested by author Faith Baldwin, "Time is a dressmaker specializing in alterations." I can accept that. But why, I'd like to know, must we long-term customers have to put up with pressed-in wrinkles? Why start with the face of all places?

Wrinkles happen when things get left too long in one place. Wrinkles are also caused by sagging. Sagging, in turn, is what happens to a body when you fail to sit up straight while practicing inertia.

The inertia that comes with growing older seldom takes root in a hurry. It creeps instead like crabgrass, crowds out middle-aged energy, and quietly weakens the ability to stand for long periods at a time. We won't mention what it does to the ability to walk and do chores.

Has anyone besides me noticed how smart we get about chores and anything else that requires movement on our part once age-related inertia sets in? There are ways, you know, to handle tedious daily jobs without losing a whole lot of sweat.

Did you know, for instance:

- that making one whole side of the bed before going around to do the other saves trips?

- that leaving stuff out means you won't have to get it out again?
- that placing the telephone to the right of your place mat means never having to leave the table to answer it? Or pass it from left to right hand?
- that radishes purchased at the supermarket don't have to be weeded?
- that stuffed animals never require litter boxes?
- that neckties and panty hose are best left for special occasions?
- that a path less traveled can be a path less vacuumed?
- that a cake baked by Sara Lee leaves no dirty pans?
- that snow on a sidewalk eventually melts?
- that the less you own, the less you have to dust?

The trouble with truisms such as those above is that less movement must, of necessity, translate into more exercise if one is to remain healthy. Even to think of additional exercise, especially when it takes longer to rest up than it does to get tired, takes more energy than most of us care to spend in one day.

Louis L'Amour hit the nail on the head when he said,

"A body shouldn't heed what might be. He's got to do with what is." Perhaps Hubert Humphrey said it best following serious cancer surgery: "My friend, it's not what they take away from you that counts—it's what you do with what you have left."

FOOD FOR THOUGHT

Inertia or not, what I have left still belongs to the God who has been kind enough to give me good health. And when the time comes for Him to give me a new body, I'll be ready.

When? Then!

It's almost a given: Celebrate the big 6-0 and, before you know it, your conversation begins to sound suspiciously like words once spoken by your parents. Could be a sudden interest in talking about the good old days is a part of our inheritance. Our own parents—or parents-in-law—do their best to hand the tradition on to us.

I discovered this when my mother-in-law was with us once on our way home from a trip. My spouse said he was sleepy and asked if I could drive. Nothing unusual about that. Except the minute we hit the high mountains, white knuckles against a black brocade handbag told me Norm's mom was not a happy traveler.

Norm dozed contentedly in the back as I maneuvered my way along number two in a series of hairpin curves. I attempted to reassure his mother. "You'd rather Norm were driving, wouldn't you?"

"That's the way it would have been in my day," she said.

I smiled as I pictured the ruts and mud, rocks, fallen trees, blown tires, and boiling radiators from her particular era of good old days. With a car like theirs, not even Norm could have mastered those mountain roads with the ease with which I drive today. According to Russell Baker, "The people who are always hankering loudest for some golden yesteryear usually drive new cars." We all tend to dredge up what's good and forget what was not while we long for what's past.

Funny how no one ever talks about riding Old Nell to the mill with a sack of grain across her rump because sacked flour was still but a kernel in some man's mind. Even in my mother's day, if you needed bread, you kneaded it. And, in more ways than one, they don't make clothes like they used to. Compared to when I was a kid, they simply make lots of them. One of my "goodest" old days happened at age ten, the day I got my very first store-bought dress. I loved and wore that dress until I grew into it, grew out of it, and passed it down to my sister who did likewise.

Houses are not the same as they once were either. Now they come with cabinets and closets and bathrooms.

Heating, if you please, can be selected through multiple choice. Choice, when it came to warming ourselves around a potbellied stove, meant which side. Back? Or front? Mid-April was about right for anticipating warm feet.

Furthermore, no matter how much our kids think I'm exaggerating or the grandkids tease, I did so, just like the postman, walk two and sometimes three miles through rain, snow, sleet, wind, dust, and mud-to-the-knees to get to a one-room school where the heating system was nearly nonexistent.

School was different back then. We learned reading, writing, arithmetic, and language skills that would last us a lifetime. By third grade, most kids could spell better than today's journalists, and we got our history straight. For fifty-five dollars a month, a single teacher taught grades one through eight, built the fire, carried in water, cleaned the building, read us the classics, taught personal hygiene, and played softball with us at recess. Our days began with the raising of the flag, the pledge of allegiance, and the Lord's Prayer. At noon, we thanked God for lunches packed by stay-at-home moms.

The school scene is one piece of nostalgia I'd like to see repeated for the grandkids. However, maybe we should first clean up the mud, install rest rooms and modern heating, and raise the teacher's salary. The past may have had its own form of beauty—but we'd be foolish to turn down the very real gifts that progress has handed us.

FOOD FOR THOUGHT

Certain things, it seems, are best *not* left unchanged. As Tennyson said, "The old order changeth, yielding place to new, and God reveals Himself in many ways."

Sleep's On

Perhaps no one understands the power of a single nap like we who are over sixty—not even small babies to whom naps are a way of life. Try nodding off into your biscuits at our age like they do, and believe me, it's not going to come across the same.

Not for one minute do I consider myself an expert on napping. For one thing, I have not had enough experience. I just think about it a lot. I've been accused of napping, in fact, when all I was doing was thinking.

Back when our house still resounded with the smack of dirty sneakers, I happened also to be a struggling young writer with too much to do and too much noise in which to try to do it. I thought if I could lie on the couch, close my eyes, and pretend I was elsewhere, the kids would quiet down, and, if I got lucky, tiptoe. Then, having created an oasis, I could dredge up scenes and bring characters (who so often behaved like my children) under control.

The ruse seldom worked. I would barely get settled before one of our young upstarts would point and snicker and holler at her sisters to come look. One of the five would then invariably say, "Mom says she's writing. Looks like a nap to me."

I wish.

In reality, the one who so graciously empties our dishwasher is also the expert on napping at our house. Name the place, and he can fall asleep in it. Being "napbidextrous," he can also read a newspaper, watch television, and nap simultaneously. Impossible? Ask the same kids who couldn't tell a muse from a nap when they saw one. It's a tale they tell to their own children. All one had to do was reach for the funnies and, with eyes as shut as a bank vault door, their father would say, "Sorry. I'm reading this paper." Attempt to switch channels and, with those same closed eyelids, he was watching TV.

The sudden need for a nap is no respecter of person, place, or time. While I don't think napping is what God had in mind when He set Sunday as a day of rest, church seems to be the place for serious nappers. As seen from the platform, the napping positions practiced by dozing parishioners must surely be a source of constant amazement and/or amusement

Pick a Sunday. Any Sunday. Like a rudderless old ship, brother so-and-so lists toward the aisle while his wife tries her best either to awaken or ignore him. Having more class than his elder brother, a senior board member remains upright, eyes closed, arms crossed, lips slack, drool on his shirt front. Men never seem to be embarrassed if caught napping, no matter how untidy their position. Women, on the other hand, tend to fake headaches and pretend silent worship. Or dig in their purses.

In spite of naps' tendency to happen at inconvenient times and wrong places, naps, like cola, can be the pause that refreshes. A nap during an afternoon of shopping, in fact, is a refreshment I wish young mothers would go home and give to their children.

Tucked center-front among the Commandments, God gifted His children with a perfect afternoon for taking a snooze. Beats me why anyone would want to use that time for shopping.

FOOD FOR THOUGHT

Naps are good. Even Jesus, while still in His thirties, took naps. Or tried to. His disciples were about like our kids when it came to letting Him. (See Luke 8:22–24.) But if our Lord needed to restore Himself now and then, who are we to turn up our noses at nap time? Naps, like all of God's good gifts, are meant to be enjoyed.

About the Author

C. Ellen Watts is the author of two missionary biographies, two young adult novels, and numerous devotionals. Her "Over 60" columns appeared in *Herald of Holiness,* and hundreds of her fiction and nonfiction articles have been published by Christian and inspirational periodicals.